Links

of

Time

Life's Memories Chained Together

Richard G. Whitner

Order this book online at www.trafford.com
or email orders@trafford.com

Most Trafford titles are also available at major online book retailers.

Note for Librarians: A cataloguing record for this book is available from Library
and Archives Canada at www.collectionscanada.ca/amicus/index-e.html

Printed in Victoria, BC, Canada.

ISBN: 978-1-4269-0809-5 (sc)
ISBN: 978-1-4269-0810-1 (hc)
ISBN: 978-1-4269-0811-8 (eBook)

*Our mission is to efficiently provide the world's finest, most comprehensive book publishing
service, enabling every author to experience success. To find out how to publish your book, your
way, and have it available worldwide, visit us online at www.trafford.com*

Trafford rev. 09/24/09

www.trafford.com

North America & international
toll-free: 1 888 232 4444 (USA & Canada)
phone: 250 383 6864 ✦ fax: 812 355 4082

CONTENTS

PREFACE

From time to time someone asks me "Are you writing another book?" Or, "When are you going to write another book?"

For those who don't know, I have written two books giving an account of my experiences in overcoming the devastating effects of grief. The first volume, *A Promise Fulfilled* deals mostly with the grief cycle relating to the loss of a loved one. For me, the loss by death of a wife has occurred twice.

The second book, *From the Darkness Into the Light*, has to do with the grief associated with an accident that changed my life forever. Generally, when anyone talks about grief, it is most often related to the loss of a spouse, child, or other loved one.

But there are other losses that can cause the grief cycle to rear its ugly head as well. It might be the loss of a job, a chronic illness, or a terminal disease. Grief becomes very real in many kinds of life-shattering events.

Working through the grief cycle is not an easy thing to do. When I lost a wife, not once, but twice, I began to wonder if I could ever overcome the anger, the sadness, the frustration, the loneliness, and the disappointment that I was experiencing.

Many people, I call them "Angels," have been extremely helpful in the process of my recovery. I never could have done it by myself.

I have found that recovery can happen, at least to a substantial degree. No matter how successful one is in reaching what is called the acceptance stage of recovery, one does not ever recover completely.

In writing the second book I drew upon some of the information in the first book. Likewise, I have turned to both volumes in completing this present book. One thing is sure! The task of writing both books has helped in going through the process of grief recovery. This has been immensely helpful in gathering my thoughts and making some sense out of what my life has become.

. The idea of writing *Links of Time,* began with the intention of showing how the events in my life followed one another as if it was some divine plan. I have proved to my own satisfaction that it has been God's plan for my life. Because of this, I have been blessed with a stronger faith and the assurance of his love and the hope of eternal life to come. What excites me most is in knowing that this blessing is available for everyone!

--Richard G. Whitner

Design
by
Devine
Will

Psalm 139 (NRSV)

(

Selected Verses
139:1, 13-16,

Lord, you have searched me
And known me.
For it was you who formed my inward parts; you knit me together
in my mother's womb.
I praise you for I am fearfully and wonderfully made. Wonderful
are your works; that I know very well.
My frame was not hidden from you when I was being made in
secret, intricately woven in the depths of the earth.
. Your eyes beheld my unborn substance. In your book were
written all the days that were formed for me,
when none of them yet existed.

Chapter One
Yes! *There Is a Plan*

In one of his presentations well-known motivational speaker Dr. Wayne Dyer once said that we come from love and we return to love; we were created in an act of love. It boggles my mind to think of how much is contained in so tiny a speck it can hardly be seen — color of the skin, the eyes, the hair, the shape of a nose — for example.

What a miraculous thing God devised in His creative spirit. His love for us is very evident when He says:

> *Before I formed you in the womb*
> *I knew you,*
> *And before you were born*
> *I consecrated you.*
> (Jeremiah 1:5)

Not only did He know us and love us before we were born, but we were consecrated for a purpose. That is, we were dedicated for a purpose with plans for our future and our hope. It says it this way:

> *For I know the plans I have for you…*
> *Plans for welfare and not for evil,*
> *to give you a future and a hope.*
> *Then you will call on me, and*
> *Come and pray to me and I will hear you.*
> *You will seek me and find me;*
> *When you seek me with all your heart*
> *I will be found by you.*
> (Jeremiah 29:11-14)

All it requires of us is to ask him. It says that if we seek him with all our heart, he will hear us and answer us.

When I recently celebrated my 81st birthday, many of the residents where I live in the Health & Wellness Assisted Living section of the retirement community told me I was just a kid. Most of them are in their mid-eighties or older. In my position as the leader of the community's Resident Council, I have had the opportunity to hear many interesting stories about people's lives.

This set me to thinking about the events and accomplishments in my own life. Almost every event of any consequence that has happened in my life has become part of a pattern like links in a chain. Because the events in my life are all part of God's plan, I call them God-incidents.

Why do I call them God-incidents? First, because they have been part of my life from its beginning; secondly, they form a very distinct, repetitive pattern which only He could create.

Chains can be a bad thing. They have often been used to bind up someone or some thing. I used to keep my cocker spaniel chained up during the day. Prisoners have been known to be kept in chains.

Chains can be beautiful things, too. A gold chain attached to a special charm or a sparkling diamond, makes any lady feel special, loved and adored.

My *Links of Time* is a combination of both good and bad. These "links" come in two colors – "light" and "dark." I like to think of them as the mountain tops of happiness and the deep valleys of despair.

As you come across some of the "links" in my story you will see how the happy, joyful, and successful times often alternate with the sad, disappointing and depressisng ones.

Any chain has a beginning and an end. The beginning of my *Links of Time,* by definition, began with my birth. It would take a very lengthy chain to include all the links that make up 81 years of life. Concequently, I have selected a few major ones to write about in depth, with mention of some incidental ones in between.

This is my story of how God's promises have been fulfilled in my life. With His help I have traveled the highest mountain tops of joy and happiness and conquered the deepest valleys of sorrow and grief. Inherent in His Word is the promise of Faith, Hope, and Love for the future, if not in this life, certainly in the eternal life to come.

In her book, *Winter Grace, Spirituality and Aging,* Kathleen Fischer writes about how memories strengthen our faith and can bring us into closer communion with God. She wrote the following:

"For faith adds an essential dimension to our reembering. In faith we not only gather our memories, we recollect our our lives before God. Our stories then take on new meaning as part of a larger story that embraces amd redeems them. Such remembering is the biblical way of appropriating the past and the basis of religious identity. At each key juncture in her life, Israel retold the story of what God had done for her, had remained faithful in the midst of her infidelities, how God had sustained her in times of trial. By remembering, she made God's love present again with power. Out of these memories arose new courage and hope that God's promises would again be fulfilled. Like Israel we tell and retell our stories, since they have levels of meaning that cannot be captured in a single telling. This way of remembering is a confession of faith.

"...in a life story, faith is the re-counting of God's presence in our journey through time. This is especially true as we age and experience our temporality more fully. The only way to capture a self extended over time is through story. And only the old can know in their own lives how an entire life cycle is a revelation of God.

"As we grow older we find it difficult to recall details like names and dates. But often we can remember key moments of our past lives, events and decisions which profoundly changed us, riches which different friends brought to us, difficulties we conquered and successes we achieved, griefs and joys we have known. These moments are more important than the details we find ourselves forgetting. Recollecting these larger dimensions of our lives before God can strengthen not only our destiny and selfworth but our awareness of God's presence with us."

Having read Fischer's work after I had wrritten most of *Links of Time*, I was pleased to see how much her words did validate my thoughts on how recalling and putting memories into print has strengthened my faith.

Chapter Two
Good Grief! What Is It?

The "links" in my life alternate between the beautiful happy times and the sad and sorrowful dark times. So, it might be useful to begin with a description of grief and some thoughts on overcoming its devastating effects in our lives.

Anyone who has experienced grief doesn't need a definition of the word. The intense sorrow they feel when a loved one dies--that's grief. Any kind of loss that brings great unhappiness, that also is grief. This includes loss of a job, particularly when one has worked at the same job for many years. Grief takes hold of one's life when a terrible accident or a chronic illness causes a complete change of life style. Simply stated, loss causes grief.

There are many ways grief affects one with loss. Grief is a process which can affect a person emotionally, physically, behaviorally, and socially. One writer has described it as a cycle of grief and says it is a process and working through this cycle becomes a healing process itself.

Elizabeth Kubler-Ross, a doctor living in Switzerland, devoted a lot of time to dying patients, studying and comforting them. There was a time when doctors didn't know what to do with terminally ill patients. They couldn't be cured and doctors had plenty of other patients needing care.

Kubler-Ross, decided to do something about this. She eventually wrote a book, *On Death and Dying*, about her work. Included in her book was the concept which has come to be known as a Grief Cycle. She identified this grief cycle as follows:

". . .stages of grief people often go through in grief recovery. These stages often occur in this order: Shock, Denial, Anger, Bargaining, Depression, Testing, and Acceptance. Her book, published in 1969 is a world classic."

Another writer refered to these stages of grief as Shock, Distress, and Acceptance.

Grief recovery usually involves going through most or all of these stages—not always in the same order. Sometimes we get stuck in one or more of the stages, longer than in others. And just when we think we have reached the final stage of **acceptance,** we find ourselves back in one or more of the other stages, with the anger or the depression and the disappointment associated with them.

It doesn't matter what has caused the loss, and suffering,. pain, and depression, whatever the disappointment and unhappiness, the devastating effects of grief can be the same. The greater the loss, the more difficult can be the healing process.

The work of going through the healing process of any kind of grief can be the same. We may experience the same feelings of anger, resentment, denial, depression, and so on that Kubler-Ross talks about in her book. After all, we are dealing with some of these feelings of loss because of the drastic change that has taken place in our lives.

Eventually, however, for most of us recovery can and does happen. The goal is to realize that what has happened cannot ever be changed. All we can do is decide to accept the circumstances we find ourselves in or decide to fret and stew, and be miserable and make those around us feel the same way. With acceptance, the bleak, useless outlook on life is exchanged for one of getting on with our lives.

Recognizing that this is easier said than done, learning to accept the fact that life is now going to be very different from what it once was, is difficult, to say the least. What it comes down to is a matter of choice.

Though I am no expert on the matter of grief, unless in the several times I have experienced and recovered from its terrible effects on my life counts, I can share what I do know. In the pages that follow are living examples of losses I have sustained involvng grief and my successes (or failures) in the recovery process. Recovery to a point can happen, that I do know.

Chapter Three
My Chain, A Beginning

On Sunday morning, May 7, 1971, I was given the privilege of taking my pastor's place in the pulpit. I chose for my text 2 Corinthians 12:1-10. I would like to share some thoughts from that message with you. The title of my message was, "What Are the Thorns in Your Flesh?"

"When I was a small child, my brother and I used to go out into the field next door. When we came back home, our socks would be full of little hitchhikers — stickers. Some times they were cheat stickers, sometimes they were little brown two-prong stickers. Whatever they were, they sure were stickery against our legs. Oh how they did hurt. In those days we wore long stockings and we would have to sit on the lawn and pull out stickers. It seemed like it took forever to get them out.

I understand there are something like two hundred species of shrubs and trees in the Holy Land region endowed with thorns. Some of them, like the acacia and the buckthorn make travel difficult.

Apparently it was a common occurrence to brush against an armored plant. Sometimes a thorn broke off, leaving its point embedded in the flesh. The Apostle Paul's readers had no difficulty in understanding his meaning when he described a source of personal vexation as a thorn in the flesh.

Quite often, the phrase, "a thorn in the flesh" became a popular reference to any vexing problem one might encounter in life. We all have burdens to bear. Someone once wrote "Life has burdens that no one can escape. Christianity does not remove the load: it teaches us how best to bear the burdens that fall rightfully to us." Sometimes the word "suffering" is used to refer to burdens or crosses to bear.

Sometimes we suffer because we are human. Our bodies change as we grow older and with that comes pain. Relationships with others change, bringing us another kind of suffering and pain.

Sometimes, because of foolishness and diso--bedience, we suffer. God forgives us, but In His scheme of things, He must permit us to "reap what we sow" someone once said.

Suffering sometimes is a tool for building Godly character. Someone likened it to a walk along the shore of the ocean. You can see that the rocks are sharp in the quiet coves, but polished in those places where the waves beat against them. God can use the "waves and billows" of life to polish us, if we will let Him.

This is the way it was with Paul. His thorn in the flesh, whatever it was, he tells us it was given to him to keep him humble. *"Therefore, to keep me from being too elated, a thorn was given me in the flesh. . ."* (2 Cor. 12:7 NRSV)

Much speculation has been made about what Paul's thorn in the flesh really was. It might have been anything from the physical — eyes, epilepsy, spiritual torment, even mental disorders, mental anguish. It could have been some sort of spiritual weakness or temptation to sin. There are those who argue that Paul's thorn in the flesh was associated with the persecution which he often experienced. We can never know for sure. If biblical scholars can't decide, who are we to worry over it?

Paul prayed three times for the affliction to

leave him. But God saw fit not to remove Paul's thorn in the flesh. Instead, he said to Paul, *"My grace is sufficient for you, for power is made perfect In weakness."* 2 Cor. 12:9 (NRSV)

Sometimes God answers in a different way. He gives us His grace so that the affliction works for us and not against us. He takes advantage of them so he can accomplish his purposes for our lives."

Dare I put myself in the same company as the Apostle Paul? Would it surprise you if I told you that I, too, have been aflicted with my own "thorn in the flesh"? As I have written above, we don't know exactly what the affliction was that bedeviled Paul. Scripture does not tell us. Likewise, it is unimportant to know what my thorn in the flesh is, either. What is important to know is that God has helped me deal with it all my life. It truly is one of the first links in my *Links of Time.*

Chapter Four
The Love Bug Bites

One of the major links in my story is money, or rather the lack of it. In my sophomore year in college I ran out of money and had to find work to enable me to continue my college education.

In 1951 I first found work in a locally owned supermarket in Sunnyside, WA, until economic conditions forced them to cut back on help. It wasn't very long, though, before I found another job on Easter weekend eight miles away at the Safeway store in Grandview, WA.

.   It was a good job. The hours were regular and the pay was acceptable, with health and insurance benefits. The employees included the manager, two of us guys, the meat department manager and two women checkers. This was in the days when stores were not open on Sundays or late at night.

I hadn't been working quite a year at Safeway when my brother Paul, a United States Marine, came home after a lengthy tour over seas. It was great to see how happy he and his wife Patricia and their little boy Jerry were to be back together.

About this same time a co-worker kept bugging me about going to the company's Annual Safeway Employees' District Banquet and Dance. Every time he asked, I would say "No." But his insistence at my going, and seeing how happy my brother was with his wife and little boy, I began to think a lot about my life. Here I was almost 25 years old, had no steady girlfriend, and no prospect of one. I soon began to wonder why it was that I had no one to love, or to love me. In those days I didn't know anything about God's plan for my life.

I certainly didn't know that God had my interests in mind when he promised that there was a hope and a future and a plan for even someone like me. And for someone who really didn't know how to pray, on a night I'll never forget, I poured out my heart to God, begging him to bring me someone to love and who would love me in return. I have prayed for a lot of things in my life since that night, but I don't think ever so earnestly as I did that time.

I spent the whole night crying out to God for help in finding some one to love and who would love me in return. I did not recognize this as any kind of grief, but the despair of loneliness could be considered a form of grief I suppose.

One day shortly after that night of turmoil, still determined to get me to the banquet, the meat market manager Howard Earhardt told me about this sweet young girl who worked at the bank down the street. She was single, lived at home with her parents, and had a new car on order at the local dealership. She comes in here sometimes on her way home after work. He promised to let me know the next time she came in.

One of my jobs was to take over as cashier the last hour of the day when the wonen cashiers went home. For several afternoons when a young lady came in, I would look across the store at Howard, but he would shake his head no. Finally one afternoon the nod of his head said yes. I checked her order, took her money, and thanked her.

I gotta tell you, I did more than "check her out" as she went out the door. Every afternoon after that I hoped she would come in. She was a slim, very attractive young lady and I began to look forward to the afternoons when she would come in again.

On a Saturday afternoon not long after, Howard stopped me as I was going by the meat counter, leaned across it and called out to the young lady standing nearby, "Norma, would you like to go to the Safeway Employees Banquet with Dick?" Taken by surprise, all the poor girl could do was stammer, "Yes, I guess so." To say I was embarrassed, is putting it mildly.

.   The banquet was a few weeks away. I thought it would be a good idea if we got acquainted before going to the big event. I finally got up the courage to call her one evening and suggested a drive for an ice cream cone or milkshake.

Well, we attended the banquet on that Mother's Day 1952, as planned. It was held in the tallest hotel in Yakima. We dined and danced and enjoyed the evening together very much.

We dated quite regularly after that. Mostly we just sat in my car in her parent's driveway almost every evening, listening to the car radio, talking and getting to know each other a lot better. I assured her mother that she could come out and check on us any time she wanted to.

I remember a picnic we had on the banks of the Columbia River south of the Tri-Cities one Sunday afternoon. I spent a lot of time cleaning both the inside and the outside of my car, wanting to make a good impression.

No picnic table around, I spread a blanket on the ground and we enjoyed a tasty fried chicken picnic lunch Norma had fixed for us. Many months later, I learned that her mother had actually fixed most of it, though Norma didn't actually say she had done it herself. I just assumed she had.

No matter, no doubt about it, this was the girl I had been waiting for. I had dated a few times before, but never anything so serious as this had happened to me. She was truly an answer to prayer. God used Howard to help Him answer my prayer!

As I explained in my earlier book, *A Promise Fulfilled,* no one was more surprised than I about these developments. Then I recalled a time when as a young teenager some of us were fooling around with an Ouija game. I asked it who I was going to marry some day. The answer I received was something like, "a girl who lives far to the east of Yakima."

It turned out that when the U.S. Government took over the area in central Washington east of Yakima, later known as the Hanford Project, Norma moved with her family to Grandview, WA, in 1943. It was at Hanford that part of the makings of the first atomic bombs dropped on Japan, ending World War II, were developed.

To suddenly receive without warning, a letter in the mail telling them they no longer could live in their homes, that the US government was taking over their land, was shocking news to receive.

It was a tragic circumstance that forced families to suddenly move from their long-established homes and farms. This is especially true when one learns that many of these farms were "soldier settlements" given to World War I veterans after the war. The veterans worked hard to develop these tracts of land into productive farms.

The residents were paid for the land, of course, but the amount was not what the land was worth. A lawyer son from one of the families successfully filed a law suit against the U.S. government, getting a better monetary settlement for the soon-to-be dispossessed families. Even that, however, was not really enough to replace a home somewhere else.

It was a "fortunate" event for me, however. Because of the atomic bomb I met the girl of my dreams. After a summer of steady dating, we made plans for a September wedding. I had really been bitten by the "Love Bug!" What initially had been the need for more school money eventually resulted in an answer to prayer for someone to love.

Chapter Five
The Polio Bug Strikes

Have you ever wished for something, hoping it would come true? I did once. Working hard all day at the supermarket, staying up too late at night was not a good idea!

If I could just stay home for a couple of days and sleep in. Then I heard the three-day measles was going around. Boy! If I could only get that, then I could get some rest. My wish did come true--sort of.

One morning I awoke with a dull ache all over. It started under my arms, gradually moving down both sides of my body. I first thought it might be an attack of appendicitis. Eventually, it seemed to be mostly in both legs.

With my doctor out of town at a medical convention I saw the doctor who was covering for him. After examining me he thought about sending me to Yakima but decided to "gamble" on one more day.

That night I went to bed hoping for some relief from the pain. As I lay on my bed thrashing around, I would move my legs up and down, all over the bed, searching for relief from the pain. As I moved my legs, for an instant the pain would stop, but then just as quickly it would return.

I didn't realize that my brother and my mother were outside my bedroom door and could hear me moaning and groaning in pain. They headed for town to find some relief for me. As they passed near my doctor's residence they saw him turning into his driveway, arriving home from the convention. He came immediately out to the house and after checking me over, gave me a pain tablet so I could sleep.

He asked me to meet him at the local hospital the next morning for a spinal tap. The pain pill worked, giving almost instant relief. However, very early in the morning after its effect wore off, I awoke and the pain was still there.

The spinal tap tested positive for the polio virus. The doctor's comment was that I had better go to the hospital for a few days

It seemed that I was about to get the rest I had been wishing for. It wasn't the three-day measles, but it was something far worse.

It was in the month of September 1952, just two years before the polio vaccine was available. I came in contact "somewhere" with the polio virus that attacked my body. I use the word "somewhere" because I never knowingly came into contact with anyone who had polio.

My mother drove me to the hospital in Yakima. It was the longest 35 miles I ever traveled all feverish and suffering in pain. I could hardly wait for the registrar to get through admitting me.

Immediately after arriving in the isolation ward the attendants began piling hot packs all over my body. They felt so good! About 6 o'clock that evening I suddenly realized that there was no more pain, but I was unable to move either leg.

All alone in the isolation ward, no family members were allowed in to see me for about two weeks. The window of my room overlooked the hospital parking lot. At least I could see my family but was unable to speak with any of them. All I could do was wave at my girl friend.

After the period in isolation I was moved into one of three rooms originally designed to be temporary psycho rooms for a lone patient. It was very small, only about 12 by 12 feet,

I was crammed in there with 17 year old Sammy and a baby crib with a small child. It was the last epidemic year for polio, and the hospital polio ward was filled to overflowing. This caused the need for using these special rooms. There was barely room for two adult hospital beds and the crib and the steamer pot that held the hot packs routinely applied to our backs and legs.

Before Sammy and I were released, however, the overcrowded condition abated and we were finally moved together into a two bed ward.

The few days in the hospital my doctor talked about, lengthened into 55 days at St. Elizabeth's Hospital in Yakima. It seems there was only one person manufacturing leg braces in the area stretching about 140 miles from Yakima to Walla Walla. The day after our braces came and we learned to maneuver about in our braces with crutches, Sammy went home to Toppenish; I went home to Sunnyside.

For most of the next three years, daily physical therapy treatments were a very important part of my life. I dreaded the physical therapy sessions at first because they were very painful.

As I understand it, the polio virus, in effect, cuts off the connection from the brain to the muscles. Without this pathway of communication, the muscles eventually begin to atrophy from disuse, and stiffen up, and no longer are able to move.

The physical therapy was intended to retrain the missing pathways and also strengthen the muscles that were unaffected by the virus. It was very painful to begin with. Eventually the muscles were loosened up and there was less discomfort to the ordeal.

Luckily, during my first year as a Safeway employee they provided us with a polio insurance policy at a very low annual premium of about $7.00 covering hospital and therapy costs. up to $5,000 or three years, whichever occurred first. In my case the three years passed before the $5,000 was used up.

I almost let the policy lapse at renewal time the second year. I became a polio victim two months later. Just knowing that all my medical expenses were covered was a big help in handling the grief I was suffering. There was also a disability policy that paid me about $55.00 per week for several weeks.

With all this going on, it is no wonder that the terrible feeling of uselessness, despair, and depression set in. Not knowing what level of recovery was in store, what the future quality of life was going to be, what my financial future was likely to end up being, all these things certainly contributed to the grief I was facing. But the most devastating thing of all, was giving up a chance of love and happiness with the one girl I had come to love more than life itself!

During those 55 days I had a lot of time to sit in my wheel chair and think about my future. It soon became clear to me that the thought of living with a polio victim was not the life for a beautiful young girl like Norma.

In my anger, I tried to avoid seeing her one day when she came to the hospital. I finally relented and came out from hiding. I tried to convince her that we should forget about getting married, but she wouldn't hear of it; said she loved me, and was determined to marry me when I was out of the hospital.

I used to jokingly tell Norma that it was her fault that I had polio. She made me fall in love with her; I couldn't eat, didn't get enough rest. Body was run-down and the polio bug was waiting to strike. Because of my own carelessness, disaster happened.

I left the hospital wearing a long-leg metal brace that allowed me to walk with crutches for a time. Later I was able to eliminate the crutches and resort to a cane. Before too long, I was even able to put the cane aside as well. Though no longer able to dance or walk up and down steps in a normal fashion, I did recover quite nicely for someone completely paralyzed in both legs for a time.

Chapter Six
Thanks Be To God

There is no question in my mind that God's plan for me included a life with Norma Eileen Skelton. He was faithful in answering my prayer for someone like her to come into my life. So when she refused to agree with me that we shouldn't get married I had to accept that this, too, was part of His plan.

When I first asked Norma Eileen to be my wife I also explained to her a life-long problem of mine — "my thorn in my flesh." It changed nothing as far as she was concerned. That is the kind of person she was.

Not only was she a kind, faithful, loving person and wife, she was a brave soul to the very end of her life. I realized that if she were willing to put up with the additional limitations I now faced because of the polio, I would do my very best to make our life together the best I knew how.

On January 21, 1953 we were married at noon by the Rev. Richard B. Stanley of the First Presbyterian Church in Grandview, WA., with my family present. My bother Paul was best man and my sister Betty was Norma's matron of honor.

None of Norma's family was there. I did not know that she had not shared our plans with them. I remember her mother telling me once that she thought we should just go off and get married.

Because of the circumstances we had decided on a small wedding in Rev. Stanley's office. When we arrived that day, however, he thought it would be more fitting if we went out into the sanctuary and he performed the ceremony there. We agreed.

Unable to drive my own car, following the ceremony, my mother drove us to Yakima to the three room apartment we had moved our belongings to earlier.

The doctors had advised me to get a sedentary job. It didn't seem very likely that becoming a classroom teacher was the appropriate thing to do, either. With Norma's agreement I decided to go to Yakima Business College and study office management and accounting.

The school's Director got me in touch with the State of Washington's Vocational-Rehabilitation program. This provided funds for retraining people unable to continue in a former line of work because of physical disabilities. After passing a required aptitude test and physical exam, my year's tuition and transportation to and from work was paid for . Until I was able to drive my car, taxi fare was paid for me; later on, gas mileage was taken care of.

The apartment was across the street from the hospital, making it easy for me to continue my physical therapy treatments. It was within walking distance of the National Bank of Commerce where Norma went to work as a teller.

At tirst bank customers shied away from this youthful teller among all the middle-age and older tellers. But soon they were standing in her line and waiting patiently.

By Mother's Day in May I was again able to drive my car. We were at my folk's in Sunnyside for the weekend. That afternoon Norma's two sisters and sister-in-law came from Grandview. I went out to the car to greet them and they all told me they thought Norma should go see her folks. I told them I had been trying all along to get her to do so.

She finally agreed to go with them back to Grandview. When we entered the house the only place left for me to sit was beside my mother-in-law. She asked me, "Aren't you afraid to sit by me?"

"Why should I be?" I emphatically replied. From that day on, we spent many weekends at Norma's folks. The four of us used to take camping trips, vacations drives and other events together. I was so glad things worked out for Norma.

All along I could tell it bothered her that she had not seen her folks in the beginning. An indication of this was a dream she had one night. She had left her sewing machine at the house when we married. She dreamed that her mother had chopped its cabinet into pieces. Eventually her dad bought the sewing machine for his wife. She actually used it more than Norma had We then bought a new machine.

Nearing completion of the college's diploma course, I was offered a job as office manager of an auto parts store in Richland WA, near where Norma's family had been forced to leave in 1943.

We both agreed that the job sounded like a great opportunity and so in February 1954 we moved to a new rental house in Richland.

Norma was able to transfer to the Richland branch of the NBC bank, and eventually became the receptionist and secretary to the bank manager.

In the fall of 1954 we began looking for a home to buy in Kennewick, WA. Richland was a government town. No one could own a home there. We hoped to build up equity in a home instead of paying rent.

In December we became home owners when we bought a new, two bedroom home in Kennewick. During the next few years we added a carport, concrete patio, and landscaped the 100 foot wide by 150 foot deep lot. Remembering how disabled I was after polio, I was amazed at myself being able to do so much. Life truly was good to both of us.

Five years later, in 1959, we sold that home and had a larger, three bedroom house built by the same builders of the first home. While both houses had a full basement, the new one also had a fireplace, covered patio, and one car garage. What fun it was seeing a weed-covered bare lot turned into a completed home. It was our Christmas present to each other. We moved in on December 23 and had family to dinner on Christmas day. The lot was a 75 by 100 foot size, a little easier to take care of than the first one. The year before, in 1958, I quit my job as office manager and began work as a staff accountant for the CPA firm of Niemi, Holland & Scott in their Richland office.

In the year following the move to our new house, Ray and Mary Lou Cain, neighbors across the street from our first home, sold their home and bought the lot next door to us. Their new house was finished in the fall of 1960. We presented them with a small album of pictures I had taken as their house was being built. We had become close friends, sharing a lot of coffee and conversation over the years.

One evening he told me that the church needed tenors in the choir. He knew about my long experience in school, college, and community choral groups. I asked him, "What church?"

"West Highlands Methodist Church," was his reply. Not members of any church, we agreed to go to church with them and check things out. This was a new, three year old congregation. We liked the church, the people were friendly, and the young pastor, Robert F. Waller, welcomed us enthusiastically.

I joined the choir immediately, an association that has lasted almost 50 years. On October 16, 1960, Norma and I were baptized and became members of West Highlands Methodist Church.

Our first assignment was as youth leaders of the junior high youth fellowship. For six years we worked with junior high kids every Sunday evening except during the summer.

Chapter Seven
The Best of Times

Working with young teenagers in the church was such a rewarding experience for me that the dream of becoming a teacher, given up 15 years before, came alive once again.

To explore the possibility that I could "cut the mustard" after so many years I enrolled in a five hour anthropology class at Columbia Basin College. I earned a grade of B plus. Deciding I could be a college student again, we refinanced the mortgage on our home and in the fall of 1966 I started classes at Central Washington University in Ellensburg, WA.

I was able to live in one of the three rental trailers my stepmother Irene had at the edge of town. She only charged me $40 a month. For the better part of the next three years that trailer became my home away from home during the week. I drove home each Friday afternoon to Kennewick and back again on Monday mornings to Ellensburg.

In February1967 I slipped on a slick spot on the floor in the trailer fracturing the left femur just above the knee. The break was so close to the knee there was no way to pin it. I was placed in a full body cast for the bone to heal. After a week in the Ellensburg hospital I transferred to Kadlec Medical Center in Richland, WA.

The physical therapist showed me how to get in and out of bed, and walk on crutches in the body cast. As soon as I had mastered this hurtle I went home. A rented hospital bed occupied the corner of the dining room for almost three months while my leg healed. I was able to care for myself during the day as Norma continued in her job at the bank.

After a time of healing I returned to my college studies until, 16 months later I fell and again found myself in another body cast with a similar injury. This time it only took a day or two to remember how to get around in a full body class and I spent weeks at home again with the hospital bed in the corner until healing took place.

My former boss at Niemi, Holland & Scott, Cliff LaHue, started thinking that with all the troubles I was having, perhaps I wasn't supposed to be a teacher. He wanted me to come back to work for him as an accountant. Not to be discouraged and determined that I was going to get through this, I soon went back to Central.

During Spring quarter 1969, Mr. Kernighan the principal and the vice-principal Mr. Eierdam from Highlands Junior High School in Kennewick came to the campus to interview new teachers. I was told they had no openings for social studies and English block teachers but they would put my resume on file. I submitted resumes to almost every school district in Southeastern Washington, hoping for a job in the fall.

One Friday afternoon in mid-August 1969 I arrived home from Ellensburg at my usual time. As I was unlocking the door, the telephone was ringing. My wife was calling to tell me that a Mr. Kernighan would be calling me at 4:00 P.M. Right on the dot he called and I agreed to meet him at the school for an interview. It seems that an eighth grade block teacher decided not to return that fall and it was almost time for school to start. Mr. Kernighan needed a teacher! I could hardly contain myself when he offered me a teaching contract. And it was only about six blocks from our home!

I later learned that when Mr. Kernighan went to the administration office to look at the file of applications mine wasn't in the file. A close church friend, the business manager, quickly looked around the office and found it on someone's desk. Without his help at the right time, I might mot have been hired. Because a teacher decided not to return to his job I now had one.

I graduated at the end of summer quarter 1969 with a Bachelor of Arts Degree in Education and started teaching U.S. History and English to eighth graders at Highlands Junior High School that fall.

My intention when I started back to college was to earn my degree in two years. Because of the interruption twice of broken bones, it took me three years. Had I finished in the two years as originally planned, that position at Highlands Junior High School would most likely not have been available.

Chapter Eight
The Worst of Times

Have you ever been so happy that life seemed too good to be true? That's the way things were for the two of us. I had finally achieved the goal of teaching. I enjoyed it so much I almost felt guilty getting paid for doing something I loved to do.

It was on February 13, 1970, her 39th birthday, Norma received a telephone call from her doctor telling her that the biopsy recently taken was malignant. What kind of a birthday present was that?

Over five years before, the doctor had removed an ugly black odd-shape mole from her arm which proved to be a melanoma cancer. He carefully examined that area of her arm every time she had a check up. Now five years later, exploratory surgery disclosed melanomas throughout her body related to the original cancer.

I can't begin to write how this news affected me. The tears of sadness and despair overflowed. I sat in my chair, holding Nicky, my Cocker spaniel, sharing the news about Norma with him. He seemed to sense the sadness I was feeling.

A chemical anti-cancer drug taken for a period of time was ineffective. The medicine had to be discontinued until her blood count could be built back up to allow them to try a different one. Time was against her, however, and she was never able to have the second round of chemotherapy.

In spite of the pain Norma wanted to work half days through most of the summer. I drove her to and from work each day. Afternoons were spent resting. The doctor gave her a prescription for Demerol and I learned how to give her injections when the pain became too intense. It was almost more than I could stand to see her hurting so. She put on a brave front and wouldn't let me give her a shot any more than absolutely necessary.

Sometimes I would lie down on the bed beside her and hold her, trying to comfort her and take her mind off the hurting.

When I asked the doctor what course the cancer would take, he told me that it would eventually reach her brain. At first she would begin having double vision and then would lapse into a coma. No one could predict how long the coma would last before she died.

I was so thankful that I had the whole summer to be with Norma. I splurged on fireworks on the Fourth of July and we spent the day with her sister Dorothy's family. The kids lit the fireworks while we all sat and watched. Norma thoroughly enjoyed the display.

Dorothy, bless her heart, stayed with Norma the last few days of August while I started my second year of teaching. It was on September 2, 1970, my birthday, that Dorothy called me at school to tell me that Norma was complaining of seeing double.

Remembering what her doctor had told me earlier about how the disease would progress, I knew what was happening. I called her doctor about admitting her to the hospital. He called in admittance instructions to Our Lady of Lourdes Hospital. I arranged for an ambulance and followed it to the hospital. After she was settled in, I went home to a freshly made bed, thanks to Dorothy.

As soon as school was over each day I visited Norma in the hospital. During that summer she had been in and out of the hospital a couple of times. When I visited her each day I found our pastor Rev. Eugene Hamblen's card on the table. I so appreciated how he made it a point to visit her almost daily.

On Saturday evening September 11, 1970, Norma's parents Otis and Gilmer, and my dad and Irene all went with me to see Norma. After a few minutes, they all left me alone with her. I suspect they knew the end was near.

While gently caressing her forehead, I carefully traced the sign of the cross, praying "In the name of the Father, and of the Son, and of the Holy Spirit, Amen" Then almost immediately, she stirred slightly and was gone. Now she was free from all pain. It seemed as if she was waiting for me to come to say goodbye.

Just then her nurse came quietly into the room and in a soft voice said, "Now you have an angel in Heaven."

I had six months to prepare for this moment, but that didn't make the realization that she was gone any easier. Our life together had been so perfect; two people couldn't love each other any more than we did. The biggest disappointment for me was her not living to see me enjoy teaching after all she did to help make it possible. For most of those three years I was at college, she spent the week days alone. Without her support I never would have been able to see a most cherished dream come true.

I had waited a long time to find Norma. Life together was supposed to be for a lifetime. Now I came home each day to an empty house except for my dog Nicky. Even that soon ended when he died four months later. I missed him terribly. He was our "child" for 17 years, almost as long as we were married. Now I really was coming home each day to an empty house.

It would be natural, I suppose, to ask myself, "Why would the good Lord bring the two of us together and then take one away?" Bit I didn't! At a gathering at the house before the memorial service for

Norma, her uncle commented somewhat sarcastically,, "Well, I guess all her church going didn't make much difference, did it?"

I didn't bother to reply. I do not believe it was God's plan to bring the dreadful cancer into her body. What I do know, however, is that "all our church going" did in fact, prepare us for facing the ordeal with the assurance of God's love!

Church family members, school co-workers, Norma's family and my family more than filled the church for the memorial service. Over 35 were served dinner by the women of the church. What a beautiful tribute this all was in Norma's memory.

```` My second year of teaching had barely begun when all this happened. After a couple weeks of getting myself together I returned to my classroom. Though not nearly recovered from the grief I was experiencing, I managed to handle the day-to-day duties of teaching. After a day of working with young active teenagers, going home to a quiet house each afternoon was a welcome change of pace.
````

Chapter Nine
Helping Hands, Healing Hands

My book *A Promise fulfilled* has the subtitle *How God Uses People*. It tells the story of the many friends and relatives, who by their love and actions, helped me recover and learn to accept the life I faced without Norma beside me.

Norma's sister-in-law Mary Jane, wanting to be helpful, invited me to a high school football game a few weeks after I went back to work, even suggested a friend to go along. Marji Parker was a college teacher and had recently lost her husband to a sudden illness. We did have some things in common, obviously.

I don't believe Mary Jane had anything permanent in mind for the two of us. She saw two people in the throes of grief and wanted to ease the burden of pain for each of us. I will admit that the thought of something permanent developing between us was an intriguing possibility.

We continued to see each other fairly regularly for a while. Marji had two young sons and after seeing them settled in bed for the night, we spent some quiet evenings listening to classical music, another interest we both shared. She had a Community Concert season ticket so I scurried around to get a ticket so we could go to one of their concerts together.

She invited her husband's folks and me to a home cooked dinner one time. It was my first and only experience at tasting escargot.

We took several Sunday afternoon drives to the countryside. We took the boys to see Ice Harbor Dam on the Columbia River. Another time we visited Don and Mary Jane's farm north of Pasco. The farm sits at the edge of a bluff overlooking the Columbia River. Marji and I walked out through the fruit orchard to check out the view.

When the passenger train line from Pasco to Prosser was closed down permanently, Don took his boy and Marji's two sons on the last trip it made. Marji and I drove to Prosser to bring them back to the Tri-Cities.

I am not sure just how much benefit Marji received toward healing from her loss with these experiences, but I know that it was helpful to me.

However, I also know that any serious relationship developing between us was not likely to happen. It was too soon after our loss for both of us. I also realized that I was not quite ready to take on a life with two young boys.

To my own surprise, I dated a couple of other very nice women about the same time. I guess I really wasn't too interested in any serious involvement at the time, however.

Another good friend, Patsy Gramling Dixon invited me to sing with The Battelle Music Makers, a company choral group sponsored by the Battelle Memorial Insitute's Laboratory on the Hanford site. She had been the choir director of the church choir when I first started singing in it. Now she was directing this group. She offered to pick me up each week for the rehearsals. Having lost her first husband in a tragic accident, I am sure she knew how comforting and healing musical activity can be. Life was beginning to be better for me, because of this.

There are times, however, when depression sneaks in, in spite of the good intentions of others. In my first book, *A Promise fulfilled,* I wrote the following:

"It's been said that time heals many things. Those of us who have lost a loved one can agree to a point. But most will also say that you are never completely healed.

The lyrics of a special song, or a memorable spoken word, or the sudden whiff of a familiar perfume, will trigger a nostalgic moment. "

Another good friend, my Pastor Leon Alden about this time encouraged me to become involved in a lay speaker training class he was organizing.

A group of us spent three weekends studying practicing and learning the beginnings of speaking from the pulpit in the pastor's absence. This soon became an important ministry in the church for me. Eventually, I served as the District Director of Lay Speaking, and later the Conference Director of Lay Speaking Ministries for the Pacific Northwest Conference of the United Methodist Church for many years.

Planning for and training lay speakers to fill local church pulpits when the assigned pastor was away was part of the job. Advanced training opportunities which lead to Certified Lay Speaker status, were developed, as well.

National gatherings of Certified Lay Speakers were held periodically in Nashville, TN, I was able to participate in these quadrennial events, meeting with Directors of Lay Speaking Ministries from all over the United States.

These are some of the people--a relative, a concerned friend, and a pastor, who helped me in a time of need, just when changes in my life needed a boost.

It was about this same time that another change was about to take place. I casually remarked to my brother one day that I might some day sell my home and buy a mobile home. An acquaintance of his in Sunnyside was planning to get married and move to Kennewick. My brother told the couple I might want to sell my home. The next thing I knew, the future husband was knocking on my door. My lawyer took care of the necessary legal documents and I soon had to scurry around to buy a mobile home before school started in late August of 1971.

I purchased a new 12 by 72 foot mobile home, with an expando unit and located it in a new mobile home park in West Kennewick. It came with furnishings so I had to sell most of my own household goods.

I lived in that mobile home from late August 1971 until April 1972. Later that year I sold it to one of the builders of the first two homes I had owned in Kennewick. He and I both were amused to think that 25 years later he was buying a home from me. It was moved from the mobile home park to within two doors of our first home.

If I had known what was about to happen next in my life, I could have saved myself a lot of trouble.

Chapter Ten
An Unexpected development

I was making progress toward living a "normal" life once again. Not actively planning to be involved in another relationship, but plans have a way of changing. The library secretary Norma Lee Jones-- yes, another Norma, and I became better acquainted.

One of my learning goals for my students was to teach them research skills. We spent a lot of time in the library. Both Mrs. Riesenweber the librarian, and Norma Lee Jones, the secretary, were helpful to me and my students.

At the end of my first year of teaching I quickly learned how seriously Norma Lee took her job. A check out sheet signed by the library was required before we could officially leave school for the summer.

"I can't okay your summer check out sheet!. You still have some books checked out from last winter!" she emphatically stated. Not until I showed her that the books were back on the shelf would she check me out! This was my first encounter with Norma Lee Jones.

As the next school year moved along, however, we became better acquainted. She invited me to a Memorial Day picnic where I got to meet some of her extended family. I really looked forward to that outing, especially when she said she was going to make some homemade ice cream. When she said it was going to be peanut butter flavor, my enthusiasm dropped. However, I soon changed my mind. It was good and the only kind she ever made as long as we were together.

On many Friday or Saturday nights thereafter we played pinochle or Marbles with her brother

Shorty and his wife Linda. These evenings with her brother and his wife soon became a regular activity for us.

During the school year if I happened to be in the library with one of my classes, Norma Lee would quietly say, "Shorty wants to know if you want to play marbles Friday night?" It never was "Would you like to play marbles?" It was always "Shorty wants to know. . ."

Sometimes I would buy a couple of steaks and take them to her house and she would cook dinner for the two of us.

Sometimes she would invite me over in the evening for tapioca pudding or a piece of made-from-scratch butterscotch pie. I really couldn't turn that down could I? What is it they say about the way to a man's heart is through his stomach? It's a strange thing, though, I never saw much butterscotch pie after we were married. Something about too much sugar for me, she thought.

During the summer of 1971, Norma Lee had an opportunity to vacation in Hawaii. While she was enjoying fun in the sun, I was "slaving away" in summer school, working on my Fifth Year studies. I later learned that the trip to Hawaii was as the guest of another man and his young daughter. Norma Lee was sort of a "nanny" during the day. She also used the trip to help her decide whether it was going to be him or me. Lucky for me, I won.

Christmas 1971 was a different experience for me. Norma Lee invited me to her house for dinner and gifts with her family on Christmas Eve. I couldn't believe the size of that pile of gifts under and around the tree. What a time everyone had opening all those gifts! I should have known that Christmas was going to be like this for years to come.

My gift for Norma Lee was a bottle of Channel No. 5 perfume. I put its small box inside of a slightly larger box; that one inside of a larger box until I had about five packages each one inside of the other. The outside was wrapped. I asked Norma Lee to put a bow on it for me and put her name on it and she put it under her tree. This happened several days before Christmas.

I didn't know she would keep the box. That box, in its original outside wrapper was exchanged between us for the next 31 years.

Between January 1971 and April 2, 1972, what began as a casual friendship of Friday night pinochle or marble games grew into a more serious relationship. On Saturday night, February 5, 1972, after getting up the courage, I asked her what she would say if I asked her to marry me. Before she gave me an answer, though, I told her of my "thorn in the flesh" problem. She thought about it for a while, and finally said, "Yes!"

Next, I suggested we get married during school spring vacation the first week of April. It took some convincing but Norma agreed about that also.

When the principal Mr. Kernighan heard we were getting married he said to me, "I thought you were spending an awful lot of time in the library,"

On the Monday morning, following my asking Norma Lee to marry me, some note cards began appearing daily in my school mailbox. These cards were typed poetry written to me. There are about thirty of them and they are a very precious keepsake I'll always treasure.

In 2005 I came across these long-forgotten notes among other papers in the den of my home. I almost disposed of them until I realized how precious they were. I gathered them into a small booklet given to family members to read and learn how poetic their mother and grandmother was. The very first one lists most of the times we dated from the beginning.

[Times we dated:]
January 1971, May 3, 1971,May 31, 1971,
May __, 1971 July 4, 1971,June __, 1971,
Aug-Nov 1971   Dec 1971Dec 24, 1971,
Dec 25, 1971 ,Jan 23, 1972, Jan 30, 1971
Feb 4, 1972,   Feb 5, 1972, Feb. 6, 1972. (3/6/72

I have chosen a few special ones, beginning with the very first one she wrote and ending with the last one I received before the day we were married. The final three lines are very appropriate as they support the message I have tried to convey within the pages of this book –the message of Faith, Hope, and Love.

(The First Poem)
My love for you could never be.
More real than it is today,
Like you, I'm waiting patiently,
When you come home to me to stay
All dates of the past,
That caused this to be,
Are added to the bottom,
For you to see.
(2/6/72)

Think hard my love, for it is known
That man gets caught when not aware,
And you should know that I do care.
And would like you for my very own!!
(2/9/72)

The secrets you've told me
have not changed my mind.

- 46 -

But made me more sure,
that your love is mine.
I will try even harder
my dear to please.
And know the results
Will grant me a squeeze!
2/16/72)

Every time I think of you
My heart goes in a spin
I just sit and wonder dear,
Where ever have I been.
Now that you have shown to me
That love is with you, too,
Let's begin a life anew,
Our love will bring us thru.
(2//21/72)

What is more beautiful than love, my dear?
The closeness, the tenderness I feel when
you are near.
It surpasses all that life holds you see,
For this is the love between you and me.
Forever we'll keep it in high esteem,
And daily fulfill our every dream.
But a never ending love we'll forever hold,
For it will always be new, but never get old.
(2/22/72

The days are passing, and the date
Is closer dear, it's only eight!
Tomorrow it will be just seven
One day closer to our Heaven.
Each day we move on up the way,
A sweeter path no man could tread,
There is a rainbow at the end.
It's full of love for us each day.

(The Last One)

Confession

From May until April, and all thru the year
Each day of it passed, as you became dear.
You didn't know just how I felt
And I couldn't tell you, either, you see.
For I wanted to know where your feelings were,
And not change your love from there to me.

At Christmas I knew my feelings were strong,
But I didn't admit it for fear I was wrong.
But each time I was with you, I knew right along,
That living without you could surely be wrong.
So hope kept me wishing that somehow you'd see
That the love we were hiding just had to be.
Then one evening, on a Saturday night,
You asked me the question, and I said
"Alright."
From that day on, we've planned for the
future,
*With **Faith, Hope** and **Love**, all bound*
together.
Because of our feelings and love for each other,
We'll go on ahead with a full life together.
                                        --Norma Lee Jones

Shortly before our wedding day, Norma Lee transferred her membership from the First Christian Church in Kennewick to West Highlands and we began making plans for a small family wedding.

But Pastor Leon Alden said, "Now you know, Dick, all of your church friends will want to be there." And they were! Members of all our families, including school, church and many friends more than filled the chapel out into the hall on Easter Sunday evening April 2, 1972, Norma Lee's birthday.

Teresa was her mother's matron of honor: Bob gave his mother away, and my brother Paul was my best man for a second time.

When my first mother-in-law, Gilmer, heard I was getting married, she told Mary Jane, "Dick said he would never get married again." Mary Jane told her that sometimes when people have had a happy marriage they are willing to try again.

And it's true. I had no intention of ever marrying again. But, after seeing how everything seemed to fall into place, how could anything have been any different? There must have been a reason things turned out the way they did. I am sure it was supposed to be that way! Once again, I believed God was fulfilling His plan for my life.

What kind of a lady was Norma Lee? She was a perfectionist for sure. For things to be right for her meant everything had to be orderly, a place for everything and everything in its place. She herself was an orderly, driven individual. Every room in our home was an orderly, neat, uncluttered place—except one. That room was the one called my den. She seldom ventured into that room because the piles of books, papers, and the like drove her to distraction. That's because I was working on more than one project at a time, I suppose. I knew where things were most of the time, though.

Any job, project, or activity she worked at was done to a standard that would make any one proud to behold. As far as she was concerned, anything worth doing was worth doing well!

Norma Lee was a woman with a big heart. She loved her kids, her grandkids, and though she didn't live long enough to really enjoy her great grandchildren, she had the opportunity to know each one and love them dearly.

She began adult life studying to be a teacher.

Although she was not able to finish her college studies, she was able to teach for several years in South Dakota, first in a small country school.

Her work as a library secretary brought her closer to being a full time teacher.

Though "they" all said it couldn't be done, she successfully taught a Sunday school class of twelve to fifteen, three and four year olds for several years. After her retirement she often spent time in granddaughter Tana's classroom grading papers and the like. Tana's students called her Supergrams.

When Norma Lee and I married, instantly I was a father, a father-in-law, a grandfather and a son-in-law. Norma's daughter Teresa and her husband Terry had a son Tod and a daughter Tana. Norma's son Robert, was a student at Central Washington University, my alma mater. Her mother Elsie Marie was my new mother-in-law. My life was full and complete.

Chapter Eleven
We'll Get Through It

In the fall of 1971 Norma Lee had a new home built on Edison Street in Kennewick. After the wedding I moved my belongings in. Moving from a 12 by 72 mobile home was a bit of a chore. The worst part was moving my library of several hundred books.

Bob and his friend Alan Hensyl moved them for me. This was the second time they had done this. When I sold my house in 1971, they had moved them to my mobile home. They "enjoyed" this job so much, that they both "hoped" they would never be asked to move those books ever again.

Her home soon became our home. We lived in this home almost 32 years. During that time we land-scaped the yard, added a large covered patio and store room, created a family room out of the garage, added an addition containing a large master bedroom and bathroom, and remodeled the kitchen.

Various positions of ministry at the local, district and conference levels of the church continued to be of interest to me. Norma was involved in the Sunday school and the United Methodist Women's group.

We traveled quite a few times to her Garrison National Family Reunions held in Springfield, Missouri every four years, sometimes stopping in South Dakota to visit relatives either going or returning. We traveled to California, and made many trips to the west side of the state visiting relatives and friends. We took two ocean cruises. One was a 25th Anniversary gift from the kids.

Norma Lee worked as the school librarian's secretary for 25 years until her retirement in 1990. After 23 years as a classroom teacher, I retired in 1992.

Watching the family grow and grow up was an especially happy times for us. Tressa Lynn joined her brother Tod and sister Tana a couple years after we were married. Many Sundays we took them to Sunday School with us. All three seemed to like staying at Grandma and Grandpa's house fairly often.

All three were excellent students in school. We were pleased to see them all earn college degrees.

The birthday and holiday celebrations were an important part of our lives. Every year for at least 30 years, we hosted the family for dinner and gifts on Christmas Eve, just like that first Christmas Eve I spent with them.

Norma's greatest pleasure was in decorating the house for the holidays. Most years we had at least two Christmas trees in the house. Over the years we accumulated an entire closet of Christmas decorations, some overflowing into the store room outside. If Norma could have her way she would put up the tree the day after Thanksgiving.

She liked white flocked trees. One year I talked her into our buying an artificial tree. She was agreeable as long as I assured her that once in awhile she could have her flocked tree. Wouldn't you know? We never had one again because she could always put the boxed tree up earlier than a real one. I must say though, she never put it up as early as Thanksgiving. I also must add that usually the second tree was a smaller real tree displayed in the family room.

As one can easily tell, our life together was rich and full. Oh, sure! We had some disagreements. It would be untruthful if I said life together was always perfect. Sometimes a disagreement over some matter caused us to question just how compatible we really were. It's like Gordon Smith, Minister of Pastoral Care for the huge Riverbend Church in Austin, Texas, said of its founder Rev. Gerald Mann after his wife died, "They were good for one another. They really complemented each other with their different temperaments."

Rev. Mann and his wife had another saying. When some difficulty arose one would say, "We'll get through it!" and the other would respond with "Or, we won't!"

Norma Lee and I worked together on projects around the house. We often cooked meals together and shared housekeeping duties.

When medical problems occurred, one of us always took care of the other. In April 1987 Norma Lee's trip to the doctor for bronchitis ended up as an emergency helicopter ride to Spokane for triple bypass open heart surgery.

Teresa and I stayed with her Uncle Wayne while there. Norma was kept in the hospital a few extra days while I came home to check on things. I discovered our house had been broken into and burglarized. The VCR, a small amount of cash, and some gold jewelry was missing. The culprit was later caught but little happened to him because he became an informant for the police.

Norma recovered very well from the surgery after an adjustment in some medication they had sent home with her.

Because of the weakness in my left leg from the polio episode earlier in my life, I broke a bone or pulled some ligaments, or cracked the kneecap several times. I also had triple bypass open heart surgery in 2000 and have had no problems from that episode since.

Norma tripped in the driveway one night, cracking her hip bone. That required surgery to repair. She suffered through cranial bypass surgery one week; two weeks later had carotid surgery. Back problems were painful. She also had a lung problem, pulmonary fibrosis, to deal with. An old x-ray revealed the fact that she had it five years before and no one had told us about it. The specialist who diagnosed it said there is no cure, but its progression could have been slowed if it had been treated earlier.

Life for almost 32 years together was a series of joys and happiness, sometimes pain and sorrow — the usual kinds of things married couples go through. We shared the joy of family gatherings, playing games together, and celebrating milestones in everyone's life. I can't repeat it enough, without a life with Norma Lee, my life would not have been so full and satisfying.

Chapter Twelve
Or We Won't

On January 20, 2004, Norma Lee had reached the limit of endurance and said, "I just can't go on like this. The pain is too much. I'd rather be dead!" The back and leg pain she had been suffering for months had become unbearable. I tried to give her some comfort by seeing that she got a lot of rest.

After trying to reassure her that "being dead" wasn't really a good option, I said, "Well, you have two choices: you can call your doctor, or go to the ER." She called the doctor and was told to go to the hospital emergency. A good friend, Lee Nitteberg, drove us to the ER at Kennewick General Hospital.

After many routine tests, her doctor gave instructions to admit her over night. "Over night" turned into several days. Keeping her oxygen level up seemed to be the most critical problem.

Finally, on January 24, a Saturday afternoon, she took a turn for the worse and was rushed into ICU where they intubated and heavily sedated her.

When I left her that Saturday afternoon before all this happened, I didn't know that would be the last goodbye I would ever be able to say to her.

Her oxygen level continued to fluctuate, first up to acceptable levels than dropping below. By Monday morning we were told that if acceptable oxygen levels could be maintained, they could remove the intubation tube to see if her oxygen level would stabilize. However, if it did not, re-intubation might be necessary, which often is harder to do a second time. Also, tests seemed to show that Norma Lee had either had a slight stroke, or heart attack and another one was likely. After hearing this, Teresa, Bob, and I agreed that after a waiting period to see if the oxygen levels stayed up, the intubation would be withdrawn and we would hope for the best. Finally, early afternoon on January 29, the tube was removed and after about ten minutes, Norma Lee quietly died, surrounded by her family, her good friend Erma, and Pastor Ed Branham. Son Bob was gone home to Issaquah overnight to take care of some important matters.

Events had not turned out the way I was so sure they were going to when she entered the hospital. I was confident she was going to be all right. Not being able to say goodbye was especially difficult for me.

Honoring Norma Lee's wishes, her memorial service was held in the mortuary and not the church. The chapel was filled to overflowing. Pastor Ed Branham suggested that we all write some thoughts to be read at the memorial service. The following quotes come from those words.

> "I don't know how, but every birthday, anniversary and holiday were remembered with cards and gifts. She diligently labored lovingly to restore our memories with photo albums, beautiful cross stitch pieces and hand made quilts preparing us for this day. Leaving so much of herself with us is comforting to us all in her absence." – Daughter Teresa

> "Mom made sure my sister and I received the knowledge of Our Heavenly Father and his eternal love. Now this gives us strength today knowing she is in God's hands and we have another beautiful soul in heaven to hear our prayers.." --Son Bob

."Being a new a mom, I feel so privileged to have known the deep, unconditional, undying love she gave her family, because now I can pass that love on to our son" –Granddaughter Tana

"The amount of love and support she has given to me and my family is more than enough to last a lifetime. I will miss her and her caring spirit. However, I will be at peace, knowing that she is healthier and stronger now as she walks with the Lord. I love you, Gram." –Granddaughter Tressa

" The memories I have, though, will always re-mind me how much she [Auntie Norm] meant to me, how big a heart she had, how much I loved her and that she will always be a part of me." – Nephew Donald

"For those of us who took the time to really know Norma, you saw her follow the two great commandments of God, She loved the Lord will all of her heart, mind, and spirit. And it showed through in the giving of her time to help others." –Close friend Larry Roberts

"I thank God for His plan that brought Norma Lee and me together and allowed me to have her with me for all these years.. To each of you, family and friends, I say Thank you from the bottom of my heart." — Husband Richard

The thoughts written above were those deliv-ered at the Service for Norma Lee. Each one was the work of the writer. Pastor Ed Branham read those by Richard, Teresa, and Bob. Tana, Tressa, Donald, and Larry each showed the courage to speak from the heart themselves.

Several other people came forward at the service and shared some beautiful thoughts and remembrances of Norma Lee. Kandie Webster,

Norma's neice. spoke, in addition to singing for her aunt's service.

Others who couldn't attend, called and offered their condolences to us. And the cards! Wow! We received well over 125 beautiful expressions of love and concern for us.

My sister Marianne, living out of state, called and tearfully told me that at exactly 1:00 p.m. on Tuesday afternoon she sat down with her husband Bill, lit a small candle, and read some scripture, particularly *The 23rd Psalm*.

Just knowing that so many people loved Norma Lee and cared enough to remember and support us has made this difficult time much easier. Someone later remarked to me about how upbeat the service was.

I now have two ladies named Norma residing in the same cemetery, one at the west end and the other at the east end. Both, I am happy to say are with our Lord, as well.

Once again I was facing life without someone who had given my life meaning and purpose. Having gone through the experience before doesn't make it any easier a second time. I later learned that she told her friend Erma that she knew she wouldn't be going home. After almost 32 years together, it was going to be difficult to deal with life all alone once more.

This time was much different. No longer working, each day began with my waking up to an empty house, except for my Shih Tzu dog Saydee Tzu. It wasn't very long, however, after Norma was gone that she began to know something was wrong.

I suppose she thought Norma Lee was on one of those short out of town trips with her friend Erma.

But as the days lengthened into weeks, Saydee Tzu gradually became more listless, didn't bother to ask for treats, finally refusing to eat altogether.

On a Friday afternoon March 12, I took her in to see her favorite veterinarian who decided to keep her over night. The next day he called and said her kidneys were failing and he put her on intravenous medication. By Sunday, the kidneys had failed completely. Dr. Privette agreed to meet me that afternoon at his office to put her down.

I then asked Saydee Tzu's favorite next door neighbor O. J. to go with me. He was like a second "papa" to her. When we walked into the room where she was waiting in a kennel, her eyes lit up as if to say, "Have you come to take me home?" It was a look that will be etched in my memory forever.

Her doctor brought her out and gently laid her on the towel waiting on the sterile metal table. I stood there comforting her, touching her nose with mine like we so often did, stroking her back, and told her that I loved her. She raised her head in recognition of O. J. then turned back toward me and seemed to sense that relief from the pain she was suffering was about to gently go away.

Dr. Privette carefully took hold of the IV and slowly injected the medicine that would send her off to that place where all animals go when they leave this earthly existence. Soon the still, motionless body told us that she was indeed gone. The doctor's stethoscope confirmed what we already knew. After a few moments of chit chat about what an intelligent, caring, loving member of our family she had been, O. J. and I turned to leave.

It was several days before I got up the courage to go back and retrieve the small urn containing her ashes. Before all this took place I used to wake up early in the morning worrying about what would happen to her if something happened to me. She took care of the problem herself, it seems.

The family assured me they would take good care of her and I knew they would. But they would treat her like the dog she was and to us, she was our baby.

Shortly after this happened two sister-in-laws died. My brother Paul's widow, Patricia, died in Sunnyside, WA; the first Norma's sister-in-law Mary Jane died from Parkinson's disease.

Not surprising to me, caring friends and family members wanted to help ease the burden I was facing. Just knowing that the family I acquired when Norma Lee and I married was available whenever I needed them, was a great comfort.

A New Turn of Events

"I consider that the sufferings of the present time are not worth comparing with the glory about to be revealed to is." Romans 8:18 (NRSV)

Chapter Thirteen
How Much Can One Take?

Time is also a good friend. It has a way of helping us recover from loss, hurts, and the lonely feelings we experience in those times. And so, almost a year and a half later, in the summer of 2005, things were beginning to be better. As I have said before, we can never fully recover the loss we experience, no matter how hard we try. We can, however, learn to go on when we have to.

A few months after Norma Lee died, a church friend named Richard also passed away. He had been suffering for some time with Alzheimer's disease. His wife Mary Alice and I suddenly had something in common. It seemed only natural to give each other a comforting hug the first few times we met at church after that.

Months later on, I was pleased when Mary Alice accepted an invitation to go out to dinner one evening. The conversation flowed so easily that the evening was over before we realized it. In fact, the restaurant had to ask us to leave. It was closing time.

Because of our friendship, recovery from the loneliness and despair and feeling of uselessness began to wane. Without her realizing it, Mary Alice helped in my recovery from grief in a very significant way. I like to think it was helpful to her as well.

On August 9, 2005, in the middle of the night, my world was suddenly changed forever. I fell in the hallway outside my bedroom door. I was pretty sure that my left leg was fractured once again.

My initial assessment of the situation was not to worry. I had fallen and fractured bones before. The doctors would take good care of everything and I would soon be as good as new!

But this time things were different. After so many years of "beating up," my leg was in sad shape. The doctors confirmed the fact that I had fractured the femur above the knee and also diagnosed osteoporosis in the leg. The bone was so thin they advised against any surgery to repair the break. The only hope was that my leg would need to heal by itself.

After some time in rehab I was able to transfer from the bed to the wheelchair and back and take a few steps with a walker. On August 19, I moved from the hospital to the Hawthorne Court Assisted-Living community. I was awakened late at night on September 1, shivering and shaking. Unable to stop, I called for help and ended up going back to the hospital with a serious infection at the sight of the fracture. Medications for pain and the infection were so strong that I was easily confused -- I was seeing writing on the wall opposite my bed. Any progress in learning to transfer and being able to stand came to a halt--completely impossible at first.

For most of five months at Canyon Lakes Rehab, I spent time recovering and gaining strength so I could move back to Hawthorne Court.

While all this treatment and care was going on I was back and forth between two hospitals and Canyon Lakes Rehab. It wasn't long before frustration and anxiety about my future began to affect my outlook on life. In all honesty, I didn't care if I lived or died.

In the beginning, it was a struggle just to pull myself up to a standing position even for a few seconds. I didn't think I would ever be able to stand again. Bill was a patient man. He let me take my time and eventually it became easier to practice standing up and sitting down. Then little by little, one step at a time, I finally managed to walk a few steps between the parallel bars.

Then one day he came in and said we were going to go for a walk -- OUT IN THE HALL! Oh! Boy! What a challenge that is going to be, I thought. It was another struggle at first. Using my walker, I would go about 15 feet, slowly at first, sit down in my wheel chair being pulled behind me. After awhile I ws making it down the hall with less stops in between. Eventually, I was going about 300 feet a day.

Believe it or not, the day finally came when I actually looked forward to physical therapy. All the hard work paid off.

Moving to an assisted-living facility was the next step in my physical recovery and rehabilitation. On January 31, 2006, after a lot of hugs and well-wishes from the staff, I rode the Dial-A-Ride bus back to the Assisted-Living community.

I had been moving back and forth so much in the beginning that people couldn't keep up with where I was located. My pastor said, "You are a hard guy to find." So I decided to send out a letter to let people know what had happened. Part of that letter follows:

Where Is Richard?

On August 9, 2005, when I fractured my left femur in the middle of the night I landed in Kennewick General Hospital. After several days I moved to the Kadlec Medical Center's rehabilitation department,

It was there that I learned how to transfer from the bed to the wheelchair and vice versa. When I learned how to do that I moved to Hawthorne Court in the assisted living section on August 19. On September 3 I awoke one night shivering and shaking--couldn't stop. An ambulance transferred me back to KGH for treatment of a serious infection in my leg.

Heavy doses of antibiotics, Fentanyl, and morphine helped in my recovery. For awhile they caused me to do funny things, like see writing on the wall.

On September 15 1 moved to Canyon Lakes Rehab & Restoration, a skilled nursing facility.

Surgery at KGH on September 18 and 20 removed some of the infection from my leg. Then I returned to Canyon Lakes to recover, gain strength, and learn all over again to transfer, stand, and use a walker to get around.

As the end of January came, it was apparent that no further progress was going to be made. Both Bill Prue the PT and I agreed that practice walking in the hall with the walker was about all there was left to do. and further physical therapy activities would not result in further mobility. I decided that I might as well move back to Hawthorne Court— assisted living at half the cost. This I did on January 31, 2006. With all this moving about. family and friends had trouble keeping up with my location. My telephone number changed twice, as well.

I would much rather be at my own home, but that doesn't seem the best, being all alone. Someone asked me recently what I would be doing differently at home from what I am doing now. Well...just about what I am doing now.

Life has become pretty much routine. I read, play and work on the computer, go to the dining room regularly for meals three times a day. I have met many new friends, most seem to be older than I am, but interesting to talk to and visit with.

-- Richard

Assisted living is just what it says it is. Some things I am able to do for myself; some tasks I can do with the aid of the walker and the wheel chair. Other necessities of living require the help of people. I have help doing the things I can no longer do for myself — cooking meals, showering, laundry, etc.

Before too long I began to adjust to my new way of life. I have my own two room apartment with everything I own, like some of my own furnishings, books, records and tapes, and computer. I have purchased a phono/cd recorder and hope to convert some of my large collection of old lp's and cassette recordings to compact disks. That should keep me busy for awhile.

A typical day consists of eating in the dining room, working (and playing solitare) at my computer, reading the newspaper, watching TV, and visiting with some of the other residents, and the like.

What I can't do is reach for things out of my grasp, or drive a car, or just get up and go whenever I want. There is no reason to be house bound, though. Trips to the doctor, shopping, or other places are available. through the local transit system's Dial-A-Ride program. The price is very reasonable, as well.

Chapter Fourteen
The Second Time Around

My family continues to help whenever I need it. Teresa is always willing to take me places I need to go. Steve provides his van with the slide out ramp and takes me to choir pracitce and church service. He grumbles, though, when I give him gas money. Larry is ever ready to bring, take, and do for me what I cannot do for myself. Being computer literate, he gets me out of trouble when something doesn't go right on my computer. Doesn't charge me, either, I get even by buying his breakfast every once in a while.

The close friendship Mary Alice and I hve continues. She still runs errands, shops, and visits me regularly. At church dinners, for instance, she helps by carying my meal to the table.

With much sincereity, I can say that I truly appreciate all that so many people do for me. I couldn't ask for anything more than what people are already willing to do to make my life better.

But inspite of it all, the cycle of grief once more invaded my life This most recent experience has proved to be much more devastating than any of the other times I have gone through the grief process. It suddenly, became very clear to me that my life would never return to what it had once been. The prospects of living like this for the rest of my life were not very encouraging.

Words are hard to find that describe the loneliness, the feeling of uselessness and the loss of a close loving companionship. It is difficult to accept the idea that things can't be the way they once were. Realizing that the physical limitations now placed on me was going to be the "norm," learning to cope was going to be very difficult.

At Hawthorne Court, at the request of the general manager, I became involved in the forming and leading of a new Resident Council. This is the means of organizing the residents of an assisted living community separate and distinct from the facility itself. It provides a unified voice for, and protecting the legal rights of the residents. Organizing monthly meetings, helping residents in various ways, being a sounding board, and helping those who need a little bit of extra assistance has been part of my job. Some indication of the feeling that even this has been part of "the plan for my life" are some of the activities I have become involved in. Once again, it is due to what I like to think is God's using people to make his plan work in people's lives.

When I was asked, by the General Manager Gayle Andress to assume the leadership of the Residents' Scholarship Fund Committee I accepted the challenge. Many years ago residents Howard and Luella Cannon started this fund to provide a scholarship each year to a graduating high school senior from one of the three high schools in Kennewick, WA. Now in its twenty-second year, funds continue to come from the resdients of the Hawthorne Court community.

In addition to financial need, academic scholarship, school and community participation, the more important requirement is that the recipient be planning on a career in an area that will benefit senior citizens. Interviewing and selecting one worthy recipient from the many who apply is always a challenging but rewarding experience for the members of the committee.

Two years ago, as leader of the Resident Council, and with the help of Activity Director Robin and her assistant Karin, I suggested the Council sponsor an "Afternoon with Santa Claus" for the children of the Hawthorne Court staff. This activity was intended to express our appreciation for the good jobs they do for us. Taking pictures with Santa Claus and refreshments were provided. For obvious reas-ons, I encouraged the residents themselves to be there and watch the little children as they came to see Santa.

When I suggested we repeat this activity the next year, our new general manager, Malaura Bricker, thought it a great idea and suggested we invite the grandchildren of the residents also.

Again, I urged the residents to be part of the party. I even told some of the older ladies that "if they were good" Santa might let them sit on his lap. Our own Chef Mel is a great Santa Claus. The most rewarding delight was to actually see two of our residents take advantage of my invitation. They had their picture taken sitting on Santa Claus's lap. One of these ladies just recently celebrated her 100th birthday. Most people think she is between 60 and 70 years old.

Most recently, Robin, the Activity Director, asked me about starting a Bible study class. Having led several Bible study classes at my church in the past, I agreed to help get one started. At the first meeting there were a dozen people eager and ready to participate in this new activity at Hawthorne Court.

These activities are but a few of the ways that healing and acceptance has become part of my life. It has also given me a sense of purpose and helpful in my own grief recvery. How can I not believe this is the way things are supposed to be?

Having reached this point in my life, it soon became time to be realistic about selling my home. Norma Lee and I had lived in it for almost 32 years. There were a lot of personal belongings to dispose of before the house could be sold.

We tried the yard sale approach at first but soon realized that the effort of that wasn't worth the time it took. Teresa and I spent several weekends going through all the cupboards, closets, and storage room.

When we finally decided on what to keep, everything else was turned over to a person experienced in the business of organizing and holding sales of household goods for a percentage of the proceeds.

In August 2007 the property was listed with a real estate company and final sale closing took place in March 2008. The new home owners were a young couple with one child.

Needless to say, it wasn't easy to give up a home that held 32 years of life's memories.

Chapter Fifteen
Grief Relief, A Higher Authority

In this book I have covered several ways grief has come into my life. These situations include the death of my two Normas, living the life of a polio victim, and also experiencing an accident that has changed my life forever.

In spite of all these major things, I have been able to make progress in reaching the acceptance stage of the grief cycle, as Kubler-Ross defines it. This has been possible because of the help of many "angels" and a lot of prayer and meditation.

When I stopped to realize each time that what happened could not be changed, the only thing I had to do was either accept the circumstances or continue to be miserable and make those around me feel the same way. With acceptance the bleak, useless outlook on life was exchanged for one of living again.

Acceptance is difficult, no doubt about it! Something that sometimes helps is the attitude we adopt. Some time ago, a Pasco, WA, pastor Roger Herndon called it **attitude**. He says, "Attitude tells all about who you are. He goes on to say that we all have problems—things we cannot control. We can, however, choose how we respond to them."

Another thing we can do is learn to endure the circumstances. There is a passage in the New Testament *Book of James* that says the following:

"...whenever you face trials of any kind consider it nothing but joy, because you know that the testing of your faith produces endurance and let **endurance** *have its full effect so that you may be mature and complete lacking in nothing." (James 2:2-4 NRSV)*

Something else I found helpful was to take to heart a message I once delivered to the congregation of the First United Methodist Church in Pasco, WA, on a Sunday morning in 1974. Some thoughts from the message "How Do We Handle Suffering?" follow.

When some tragedy strikes us or our loved ones, we have two choices open to us. We can blame God for what has happened, become resentful--fill our lives full of hatred, taking our revenge and troubles out on those around us. Or, we can turn it over to God.

When my wife suffered the pain of incurable cancer, the first thing she asked, as so many of us do when tragedy strikes was "Why did this have to happen to me? I never heard her say 'Why me?" But I think she rather thought "Why should this have to happen to anyone?"

From the time she became a Christian in 1960 until she was diagnosed with cancer she had learned to have faith in God, assured that He would be with her during her ordeal. She was a source of inspiration to everyone, including me. God seemed to be using her pain and suffering in some special way.

Certainly, no one can really know how strong another person's faith is. One thing I am sure of, faith, or lack of, often affects how someone reacts to the hurts and disappointments and tragedies that plague them.

Yes! We can drown ourselves in our own sorrows, blame others, cry out, "Why me?" until we reach that point when we remember that God is near and ready to help. We can cry out as the Psalmist did, *"God is our refuge and strength, a very present help in trouble."* (Psalm 46:1 NRSV)

How much easier it would be if we prepared ourselves for such a day as this with the assurance that God is really with us all the time.

None of us is immune. We will face many trying times and how we react will depend on how we prepare ourselves.

The first of these thoughts has to do with the origin of suffering and the will of God. Where does our suffering come from? Is it the will of God? Many say it is. So many times that is the response given by well-meaning people in their attempts to comfort someone experiencing a tragic moment.

Some years ago in the Midwest, a parochial school burned. Several of the children were unable to escape and died in the fire. The man in charge tried to comfort the shaken parents by saying, "This is the will of God."

What really happened was that a janitor had left an oil-packed pile of rags under a stairway. Spontaneous combustion caught them on fire.

A young minister blamed himself when a small boy drowned while on a picnic outing. The minister was unable to revive the boy after pulling him from the water. He blamed himself for the accident because he was responsible for the group outing. He felt guilty for not being able to do more to save the life entrusted to him.

He was doubly troubled though, when members of his congregation said, "It's not your fault. It is God's will." "God must have planned it this way, and we can't fight His will." or "God wanted to save him from war, or crime, or something worse. Who knows why God did it?"

Some, no doubt, thought it was the will of God that my wife should feel the pain and suffering of the cancer that had attacked her body. I cannot believe that it was God's will!

God is ever ready to take such circumstances and turn them to good. We have this assurance — that when we suffer, Christ suffers right along with us. It can happen however, only if we accept it ourselves and offer it up to God as a willing sacrifice.

We must be careful, though. So often when we look back and see what good has come from some tragic circumstance, it is easy to say, "See! It was God's will after all. He inflicted suffering on us just so that some good could be brought from it." To me that would be like a father inflicting pain on his child so he could kiss him and make it better. If we give God the opportunity He will make good out of evil, but the evil is not caused by Him. When disaster strikes is the time to lean back and rest in a settled and firm belief that God can bring about his will in the end. He has shown us this in the life, the death, and resurrection of Jesus Christ.

And just as he has shown us this, so also has he shown us in the circumstances of those in pain and anxiety who feel his nearness and strength in the way they respond to adversity.

Many tragedies are the result of human choices. When I came down with polio I knew that God didn't cause it to happen. It was my own "reckless" behavior that caused it.. He did help me in my recovery and willingness to accept what had happened, though.

We, too, can face the suffering just as Jesus did Furthemore, Just as Jesus showed us, we can rely on the promise of eternal life to come.

We have a choice in how we respond to tragedy. When each of my two wives died I chose God's love and mercy to sustain me in the grief recovery process. What I have discovered is that because I chose long ago to put my life completely in His hands, He helped me to prepare for these devastating events.

We can accept whatever life brings with the assurance that *"the sufferings of this present time are not worth comparing with the glory about to be revealed to us." Romans 8:18* (NRSV)

Peter also tells us *"Since therefore Christ suffered in the flesh, arm yourselves with the same intention, for whoever has suffered in the flesh has finished with sin, so as to liive for the rest of your earthly life, no longer by human desires, but by the will of God."* 1Peter 4:1-2 (NRSV)

Reading these thoughts once again reminded me that God does care about what happens to us. By the spring of 2008, less and less often did I find myself falling into periods of loneliness and discontent. Half way into the third year of living in the assisted-living facility I was finding myself quite comfortable in my surroundings. Things were about to change, however.

Chapter Sixteen
More Than I Wanted To Know

During a routine visit to my nephrology's one day. I was handed a printed folder with the title "Freneius Medical Care" subtitled "Pre-Renal Education," that I realized that my life was about to change some more.

While waiting for Dial-A-Ride to pick me up after my appointment, I began to explore what this document meant about Freneius medical care and what its implication might mean for me. I signed up for the two meeting dates my doctor had circled. The May 20th meeting was labeled "Renal diet"; and the July 8th meeting, later changed to September 9, was titled "Treatment Options."

The following explanation was on the brochure:

Renal replacement therapy leads to lifestyle changes not only for the patient but for the loved ones as well. Pre-renal education is designed to help patients and their families make the best decision possible about the care they wish to receive once they need to start renal replacement therapy dialysis. Typically, the following subjects will be included.

1 Information on the kinds of dialysis.
2 Guidelines on the renal diet
3 Costs and insurance
4. Support available from a social worker

Suddenly I found myself looking into all the information I could find about kidney disease and what it meant for my future. At first I began to speculate on what caused me to be afflicted with kidney disease.

This possibility of my having kidney disease did not come as a complete surprise. For well over a year every monthly lab test report had some notation about a GFR reading. It usually noted "<60 indicated chronic kidney disease." This was followed by "GFR 15 indicates kidney failure". My test number result has varied between 25 and 19, the past year or so.

I had learned earlier that diabetes and kidney disease often come together. I knew that diabetes is often a "gift" handed down in one's family. Yes, I have been plagued with diabetes for years.

There is also an association between high blood pressure and kidney disease, as well. For months now I have been battling the effects of elevated blood pressure and the side effects of medication used to treat it.

The infection associated with the leg fracture, already described previously, also had affected my kidneys. It is possible that this might be the cause of the kidney disease.

The risk factors for kidney disease, it turns out, include diabetes, high blood pressure, family history, older age, and certain ethnic groups. A GFR test identifies the five stages of kidney failure. GFR stands for Glomerular Filtration Rate. This test measures one's level of kidney function and determines what stage of kidney disease one has.

When the GFR rate is 90 or less -- Stage 1, some kidney damage is indicated; a GFR rate of 60 to 89 -- Stage 2, indicates mild damage; 30 to 59 GFR shows a moderate increase in kidney damage; and severe damage is indicated when the GFR is 15 to 29. Stage

5, kidney failure is indicated when the GFR rate is less than 15.

Whether it was the infection that invaded the fracture area, the diabetes, the high blood pressure, or something else, I was now faced with the fact that I was at Stage 4. At this stage, further deterioration to Stage 5, GFR 15 or below – kidney failure can be expected sooner or later.

When my daughter Teresa, learned about the meetings, she wanted to go with me. Two pairs of ears are always better than one so I reserved a spot for both of us.

The topics were broken down according to pre-dialysis diet, diet during dialysis, the transplantation diet, food values, and hints for making the diet work.

RENAL DIET

The function of the kidneys is to remove waste and extra fluid from the blood. Impaired function makes it harder for the kidneys to do their work. As a result, the proper diet of a person with kidney disease becomes especially important.

The first meeting, May 20, 2008 was all about the renal diet. For two and one half hours about eleven of us received a lot of valuable information. A lot of do's and don'ts were covered. Included were lists of foods to consume on a limited basis and lists of those to avoid completely.

When the dietician conducting the meeting started talking about things like sodium, Phosphorous, Potassium, proteins, calories, and cholesterol I could see how complicated a diet was going to be for someone with kidney disease. Restrictions on dairy products and processed meats were discussed.

For me, living in a community like Hawthorne Court where there is only one diet, it would not be easy. For a diabetic patient it would be even more difficult.

TREATMENT OPTIONS
Dialysis

The September 9 meeting was a very informative meeting and we had a chance to see the area where dialysis treatment is carried out.

It is quite an impressive place with 11 stations, each with a comfortable place to sit or lie next to a machine. Patients can read, sleep, watch television, and other activities during the time dialysis is taking place. One patient is able to work on her stamp collection while there.

There are several options for dealing with kidney disease. Two of them are forms of dialysis. Dialysis, simply put, is the process of removing wastes and extra fluid from the blood--something the kidneys no longer can do.

Peritoneal dialysis cleanses the blood inside the body. Special cleansing fluid is pumped into a body cavity by means of a catheter inserted near the navel. This catheter must be inserted by minor outpatient surgery and stays in as long as one is on this type of dialysis.

The blood is filtered through a membrane passing the wastes into the special cleansing fluid. The fluid must be drained from the body and replaced with fresh solution periodically, about four times a day. This procedure is referred to as an exchange. An exchange can be performed in any clean area — at home, work, or while traveling.

A variation of this procedure is known as APD, or Automated Peritoneal Dialysis. The exchanges are done overnight with a machine known as a cycler.

Both of these methods offer some advantages. The patient can go about one's business and other activities with some ease while the exchange is going on. It provides continuous therapy.

Disadvantages include the permanent catheter outside the body, storage space in the home for supplies, space in the bedroom for equipment, and some risk of infection.

The other form of dialysis, known as Homodialysis, removes the wastes and excess fluids outside of the body. This is done by pumping the blood from the body into a special dialyzer which filters the blood as it passes through and back into the body. This involves having two needles, one inserted into an artery and the other into a vein, each time dialysis is performed.

Homodialysis is time consuming. For most patients this procedure requires a four hour session, traveling three times a week to a dialysis center. Other disadvantages include following a restricted diet to limit fluid intake, permanent access to the leg or arm to get the blood, and some risk of infection.

For otherwise healthy people, dialysis is a life-saving procedure to go through. However, mentally and physically it can be an exhausting time. People who have heart or lung disease, poor circulation in the extremities, those plagued with cancer and other chronic diseases, or suffering with dementia will find dialysis difficult.

Elderly people with illnesses like those mentioned above may only have a 50-50 chance of living more than a year with dialysis.

TREATMENT OPTIONS
Transplantation

The third treatment option is to have kidney transplantation. To be eligible for a trans-plantation, a candidate must meet a number of tests. One's general health must be good, the ability to work at staying healthy is necessary, and be recommended by the health team after being subjected to a number of tests.

Some advantages of transplantation over dialysis include no dialysis treatments, longer life than with dialysis, fewer fluid and diet restrictions, and the ability to work without a dialysis schedule.

Disadvantages associated with transplantation include stress of waiting for a donor kidney, requires major surgery, the risk of kidney rejection, medications before hand and forever after, and the possibility of infection.

EXPENSE OF OPTIONS

All of these options are quite expensive, especially the transplantation option. Medicare, private insurance and some state medical aid associations do provide medical financial assistance.

TREATMENT OPTIONS
No Dialysis

There is another, fourth option one can choose, a decision to do nothing at all. A decision to forgo dialysis is a choice often made by prospective dialysis patients.

When asked about the consequences of that choice, we learned that toxins begin to build up in the body. The patient gradually experiences more and more tiredness and weakness, eventually going to sleep and failing to wake up. There is no pain associated with this. Dying with renal failure is usually peaceful and is not painful and only takes a short time to happen.

Only the patient can make the decision whether to undergo dialysis or not. We have to make choices in how we want to deal with our kidney disease. We can choose a kind of dialysis that is best for us or we can decide to choose no treatment at all.

In addition to the purely physical effect on our bodies, there is a mental and emotional aspect to consider. It turns out that grief can have a very strong influence on our decision! This is especially true when we are dealing with a terminal disease.

I mentioned earlier that there was a time when I didn't really care if I lived or died. I've not spoken much about how grief can lead to this kind of thinking. Sometimes, however, there comes a time for some when life has lost all meaning. This dire outlook on the future may be the result of any number of reasons. Physical disabilities can prevent one from carrying on normal activities and a feeling of uselessness prevails. Add to that the loss of independent living, not being able to do the simple day-to-day tasks you were once able to perform. When this occurs more than once, it is no wonder that the prospects of no longer living become more attractive all the time.

When I returned to the Hawthorne Court Assisted-Living community I brought what was left of the pain medication I had been given before. In a converstion with a friend one day, with tongue in cheek, I said if things got too bad I had an easy out at my disposal.

Another time, upon hearing that some senior citisens often have to choose between buying groceries or buying medications, I comented, also. jokingly, that all I needed to do was stop taking the handful of pills I take every day.

If you remember the discussion earlier , you will recall the likelihood of my experiencing kidney failure. It was mentioned that when the GFR measure of kidney function reaches 15 or below, one is at Stage 5, considered kidney failure. A receent test showed the GFR to be 19. But the most recent test result shows the GFR had risen back up to 23.

Perhaps sooner, rather than later I will have to be making some choices regarding treatment options. I have already covered the pros and cons of "treatment versus no treatment"

What will it be for me. dialysis or no dialysis? The important questions to be considered are: "What will the quality of life be with or without treatment?" and "How long will life be prolonged?

Do I want to deal with the grief that can raise its ugly head? Grief associated with a chronic illness, especially one that sometimes ends in death, makes the acceptance stage of recovery even more difficult to reach.

Whatever decision I make, if the Links of Time as I have descvribed them in this book, continue in my life, I will have the very best "Counsel' in helping me choose what's best for me.

A Logical
Conclusion

How lovely is your dwelling place, o Lord of hosts!
My soul longs, indeed it faints for the courts of the Lord;
my heart and my flesh sing for the joy to the living God.
--(Psalm 94:1-2 NRSV)

Chapter Seventeen
A Logical Conclusion

As I sit here at the computer struggling to find the right words to write on the pages before me, playing in the background is the Mendlesohn oratorio *Elijah* Not only is the music itself inspiring with its great solo and choral renditions, but when Elijah calls on him, God answers with his mighty power. It is worth repeating that this music has been partially responsible for my Christian walk. I can't begin to tell you how it has touched my heart.

I've written earlier about singing in an oratorio society that performed this magnificent choral work. The effect this music had on me gave me my first real inkling of God's place in my life.

One of my reasons for writing this book has been to explore how the events in my life have come together and have been part of God's plan. Sometimes it has been hard to see how those plans are for my own good (welfare) and not for sorrow and sadness (evil). All that has been written so far, however, has convinced me that what it says in *Jeremiah* is indeed true.

What if the atomic bomb had not been invented and the U.S. government hadn't taken over the White Blufffs-Hanford area of the state of Washington? The Skelton family would never have moved to Grandview, WA. Then Norma Eileen Skelton and I might mever have met.

When I have taken the time most earnestly and sincerely to seek him with all my heart, he has heard me and answered me just as he has said he would.

That's what happened on that night so long ago in 1952 when I poured my heart out to God in a plea for someone to love and to love me in return. He had promised "come and pray to me and I will answer you." And He did!

What if I had not had to battle with the results of the polio bug. It led to my becoming an office manager and accountant, which in turn, led to a move to the Tri-Cities.

What if a special friend and neighbor had not introduced us to a life of ministry in the United Methodist Church, which resulted in my return to college and a life as a classroom teacher. It was a wonderful life until cancer took the life of the one I planned to spend my whole life with.

Back in those early days when we were playing around with that Ouija board another young girl was growing up in South Dakota, which of course, is directly east of Yakima, WA. If Norma Lee Jones had not moved to Washington in the late 1940's I would not have had a second chance at happiness and been blessed with a whole new family.

You know the rest. We could continue to play the "What If?" game. But, you have read how each incident in my *Links of Time* is "hooked" in some way to the other. As far as I am concerned this has all been in the plan set out for me.

Each time there has been a "dark" link in the chain, it has been followed by a "light" one. But the dark ones have not been without their purpose either. Let me return to the message on the "thorn in the flesh" to explain what I mean. Here are more passages from that message quoted earlier: "What Is the Thorn in Your Flesh"

The grace which was sufficient for Paul is also sufficient for you and me. Paul says he is content with weaknesses, insults, hardships, persecutions, and calamities for the sake of Christ.

Twenty-three years ago I was in Kadlec Hospital -- hurting. I had injured my knee and found myself in a body cast waiting for brokien bones to heal. At that time, the Central United Protestant Church in Richland, WA broadcast their Sunday morning worship on a local radio station. I obtained a copy of the pastor's sermon because his message hit home.

. Pastor Joe W. Walker's message was one about "hurts that help." The message spoke directly to me and supported and emphasized what I have been saying. One thing Pastor Joe Walker said was, "We dare risk hurt and involve ourselves in each others' lives only if we know that God loves us. Then a strange thing happens; not only do these hurts become helpful to us in the building of the nobility of our own souls, but they equip us for helping others. . .The world is in desperate need of persons who have been deeply wounded and deeply hurt and who are willing to turn back upon their path to lend a hand to those who come behind."

So, what is the thorn in your flesh? Can you turn it into a gift from God like Paul did? The thing is --those who have hurts and those who are hurting now are equipped to help each other.

Who better than anyone who has lost a child or a spouse, or has recovered from the problem of alcoholism; or has gone through the tragedy of divorce and recovered to a new life is better equiped to help others? Then, as Joe Walker said, "I have seen people who have walked the dark shadows of life and in so doing have equipped themselves for the helping of other persons."

Walker is right when he says, "Sure you hurt. Life has all kinds of hurts in it. But with God's grace and with an understanding of His abiding love, your hurts can help. They can help make you a more noble person, more a human being. And they can equip you to follow the hurts out into the world where you'll find Christ hard at work trying to stop the hurting and asking you to lend a hand."

May we all be like Paul. May we accept the grace of God and the glory of God. Paul took pleasure in the trials and problems he had because he was suffering for the sake of Jesus Christ. He was glorifying God by the way he accepted and handled difficult experiences in his life. Can we do any less?

Yes! Hurts do help! When I compare the hurts in my life with the joys and happiness that often follow them, those are the times when my faith has been strengthened. Like so many, when we hurt, that is the time we truly and earnestly seek the Lord's help. I am no different in that regard.

Chapter Eighteen
Just Luck, Or Is It Planned?

Some skeptics would say that from the way things have played out, they were all a matter of luck. But what kind of luck?

If this be true, then it must have been bad luck that I suffered with polio. So also it must have been good luck that prevailed as I recovered and nade a successful adjustment to life because of it.

If the plans for my life have been a matter of good and bad luck, then my making the right choices have been an important part of how things turned out. The Roman philosopher Senecca in 5 B.C. is reported to have said, *"Luck is what happens when preparation meets opportunity."*

That's what my life has been: preparation for making the right choices when the opportunity has presented itself. In elementary school I always looked forward to music class. From those early beginnings, the foundation was laid for music activities in jumior high, high school, and college. This, in turn paved the way for my participation in oratorio and church choir music organizations.

Oratorio and church choir music have been very important in my Christian life. They have been the preparation for me to be a church choir member, to seize the opportunity to become a teacher and church leader, as well as a certified lay speaker for Christ in the local church. So if preparation has met opportunity in my case, then I guess one could say that luck has played an important part in my life.

However, something else had to be in place for me to begin the preparation. That, for me, has been God's plan. If there is any luck in the matter, it is when I made choices in how I have responded to, and followed his plan.

` How did I do that? As I have pointed out, choir music first got me active in a church. But right away, within a month of becoming members, the Pastor Robert F. Waller asked my wife and me to take over the responsibility of leading and teaching junior high age kids about the love of Jesus Christ.

It was our choice to make. Either we could accept the assignment or not! There is an old, saying I have found to be true 'The teacher learns more than the students." Every Sunday evening for six years, except during the summer, we worked with the junior high youth group, playing, worshiping, and studying.

Can you believe that two people with no background in the Christian life were asked to teach junior high age kids all about it? A lot of prayer, study and prrepartion went into each Sunday evening's lessons. The pastor knew what he was doing when he asked us to take on this responsibility. What a great way to learn about the love of Christ! We made the right choice!

There is another way to learn to make the correct choices: be involved in the life of the church. That's what we did. Not only music and teaching, but accepting leadership positions in the church is a wonderful way of not only learning about, but also really knowing what the Christian life is all about.

There are three areas that have been my most favorite ways of involvement in the church. Music, of course, was, and always has been the most precious to me. A second avenue of service was in teaching, both in the church and in the secular world. The third activity very important to me, closely related to the second, was becoming a certified lay speaker in the church. I have already described the lay speaking program. Let me just say that without involvement in the local church none of these things would have been possible.

Have you ever watched a potter working with clay? I have not had the opportunity to see this, but I have seen the results of the potter's work many times. I understand that when working at his or her task, if something isn't turning out right, the clay is smashed down and the work starts over.

I have said before, and I continue to believe, that God does not cause bad things to happen to us. When misfortune visits us, it may seem like God is "smashing" us down but He loves us too much to do that!

What He can do is "re-work" us like the potter at his wheel. What he does do is take the circumstances we find ourselves in and make something good come from them—if we will let him. *Jeremiah* tells us how God can work in our lives:

> *The word that came to Jeremiah from the Lord, "Come down to the potter's house, and there I will let you hear my words." So I went down to the potter's house, and he was working at his wheel. The vessel he was making was spoiled in the potter's hand and he reworked it into another vessel, as seemed good to him.*
>
> *Then the word of the Lord came to me, "Can I not do with you, just as the potter has done? Just as the clay is in the potter's hand, so are you in my hand."* (Jeremiah 18:1-6. NRSV)

The Word of the Lord is enough for me to be convinced that He does have a plan for each one of us. Can you recognize what His plan has been for you?

. . . .in life, No matter what you do

all that's important is –

What's In It
For
God?-

Chapter Nineteen
God of Love, God of Promise

What does it mean "God is a God of love" or a "God of promise"? In exploring this idea of God's plan, another thought has occurred to me. What's in it for God?

Why would he care enough to create a plan for our lives? A question often asked is, "What is God's purpose for our existence?" The answer is: so he could love us!

A story is told about a wealthy couple who had everything they needed, everything that is, but children. So they decided to have a child.

"Why would you do this?" they were asked. "So we can love him or her," they replied.

I can relate to that feeling. I remember when I so desperately wanted someone to love. When I prayed for someone to love, he answered my plea. If God's plan was to create someone he could love, then no wonder he was willing to fulfill my desire for the same thing.

But more than that. I wanted someone who would also love me in return. And that's what God desires also. He wants us to be like Jesus and love him in return.

Because God is love!, Christian love is something we cannot start by ourselves. Our ability to love others is rooted in God's love for us. When we know him, we become capable of truly loving others. Not only that, when we show our love to others, we are returning that love to God, as well. We have a responsibility to repay the love which God has shown toward us.

But what does it take to let God love us? We have to learn what God is like. To know Christ is to know God. *"Whoever has seen me, has seen the Father,"* John 14:9 (NRSV)

What if, we at home, in the church, or in our social life loved people "as Christ loved the church and gave himself for her?" What would happen if we were open to follow, listen to, share with each other, the obedience we would have if we were reacting to Christ himself?"

Do you recall the story about the red box earlier in this book, the one containing a Christmas gift for my soon-to-be wife? The following account is a recent update on that true story, thanks to my two granddaughters. Christmas is a time of gift-giving. It is especially meaningful when it is founded on love. Though the event happened at Christmas 2007, the following story was part of my Christmas 2008 message to my family and friends.

Memories, Love, and Hope

Christmas is a time when we resurrect past memories that mean so much to us. These thoughts almost always include loved ones associated with them.

Christmas also means love. Love is a gift. We celebrate God's gift, in the birth of the infant Jesus. We share our love by the gifts we give to loved ones.

Christmas also means hope, hope of eternal life. Jesus Christ was born, died, and arose to show us that we, too, can do the same.

These three words: memories, love, and hope, brought to mind Charles Dicken's *A Christmas Carol* and the three spirits in the story: the Spirit of Christmas Past, the Spirit of Christmas Present, and the Spirit of Christmas Future. With apologies to Dickens, here is a story that has all the marks of a Christmas past—memories, a Christmas present—love, and a Christmas future—hope. It is the continuing true story of the Red Box.

Where's My Red Box?

In 1971, I purchased a small bottle of Channel No. 5 perfume for a special lady in my life. It was to be her Christmas gift. I put the small box in a series of boxes, each one larger than the one before, until the fifth box was about eight inches square. The lid was wrapped separately so all the paper would not have to be torn off when the outside box was opened.

I took the box over to Norma Lee's house one evening before Christmas. I told her I had wrapped this gift for some one but wasn't good at making bows. Would she please put one on it for me. After she dressed it up with a pretty bow I put her name on it and asked her to put under her Christmas tree.

After Christmas she kept the box and carefully put it away in her Christmas decorations. Then Christmas a year later, when we were married, she returned the box to me with a small gift in it. Each Christmas thereafter, we took turns exchanging the box with each other.

I have continued to use the box, still in its original outside wrapper, as a decoration and remembrance under my tree each Christmas since Norma died.

Now fast forward to Christmas 2007. Early on Christmas Eve afternoon, Tana and Tressa came by to pick me up for the evening's activities. While I was getting ready to go, Tana disappeared out to the car. When I was ready, Tressa and I joined her and off we went for the evening at Tana's house.

Christmas morning as I sat opening the gifts from under my tree I suddenly realized that the red box was missing. "What has happened to my red box?" I thought!

When Tressa came to get me for the day, I asked her, "Where is my red box?" She pretended to know nothing about it. Well, when we got to Tana's house, I again asked, "Where is my red box?" With an impish grin, Tana fetched the red box from under her tree and handed it to me. Inside the smallest container was a new wristwatch. What a beautiful gesture my two granddaughters had, carrying on a tradition that their Grandmother and I had followed for 30 years.

This beautiful act of love, keeping a memorable tradition from the past alive, confirms for me what I have known all along. Even though Norma is gone, I am still recognized as a member of the best family anyone could ask for.

Memories of Christmas Past do much to create the Christmas Present. Therein lies Eternal Hope for the future.

God's gift of love to us is like the red box. In the beginning Love was wrapped in a small babe, lying in a manger. In that gift was the most precious thing He could give us – Love, Hope, and the promise of Eternal Life.

If we seek Him with all our heart, He will be found by us. If our purpose for being is to be the object of God's love, then what?

Surely God has something more in mind than merely loving us! He wants us to live eternally with him!

The 16th century Italian scholar and poet Petrarch said this: *"The time will come when every change shall cease, This quick revolving wheel shall rest in peace: No summer then shall glow, nor winter freeze Nothing shall be to come, and nothing past, But an eternal now shall ever last."*

For the Christian, eternity is what everyone waits for. There was once a man, who on his eightieth birthday celebration dinner is supposed to have said:

"In my long life I have had many exciting adventures. I have crossed the ocean numerous times, and have been around the world. But I am waiting the greatest adventure of all, the journey into that land from which no traveler has ever returned."

People have long believed that eternal life is God's gift to us. We can't earn it! All we have to do is love Him and accept the gift he offers. In the sixth chapter of *Romans*, it says:

"...the free gift of God is eternal life in Christ Jesus our Lord." (Romans 6:23 NSRV)

Perhaps Heaven, wherever it might be, is the place where we will know how to live when we get there. Hell, it surely would be for those who wouldn't know how to act because they had never learned in this life.

The following true story was written and published by an acquaintance of mine some years ago. This story involves her small son on a visit to the hospital to see his grandfather who happened to be her father. I have her permission to tell it.

Wings For Eternity

An eight year old boy was visiting his grandfather Hicks, sick in the hospital. He was especially apprehensive during this visit, for his other grandfather had just died only two days before. Grandfather Riesenweber and Darren had shared an avid interest in rocks: hunting them, collecting them, and cutting and polishing them. And now here was his other grandfather sick in the hospital.

As they entered the hospital room, grandfather turned, greeted Darren and his mother, and held out his. hand to Darren.

"I was sorry to hear that your other grandpa died," Grandpa Hicks said. "I know you must miss him a lot." Darren nodded. His eyes filled with tears, and a big sob escaped his tightly closed lips. He was trying hard to be brave.

Being a minister, Grandpa Hicks was well acquainted with grief and didn't try to stop the tears or change the subject. He just continued holding on to Darren's hand. Then something on Darren's arm caught his eye. Grandpa turned his arm over to have a closer look, and could see that Darren had been doodling on his arm with a pen as children often do.

"What did you draw here on your arm, Darren?" "It's a butterfly." Darren said between sobs.

His grandfather traced his finger around the edges of the drawing as he said, "You know, once that butterfly was a caterpillar. One day he started acting real sick. His friends all worried about him, and gathered around to comfort him. The caterpillar only got worse, and pretty soon he covered himself all up in a chrysalis so his friends couldn't see him. After waiting a long time for him to come out, they decided that their friend must be gone for good, so they all gathered together and talked about the life he had led, what he had meant to them, and how much they were going to miss him. Then they all said their goodbyes and sadly went back to their homes.

"After a short time the chrysalis slowly began to open and out came a beautiful butterfly. It was the same caterpillar as before, only now he had beautiful wings. Now he wasn't just limited to a small branch on a tree. He could spread his wings and take to the sky. A whole new world had been opened to him. Grandpa paused for a moment. Darren's tears had subsided. He was listening attentively. The strangeness of the hospital room was forgotten as in his mind he soared through the sky with the butterfly.

"I'm not going to die during this hospital stay," Grandfather said quietly. "But someday I will die. When I do, I'd like you to remember this story, and be able to release me to my new life in Christ. It's a whole new world, and death will give me the wings I need to be born into it. Will you try to remember" Darren nodded.

There is something you can do for your other grandfather right now," his grandfather continued. "You can release him to his new life. Why don't we tell God we are just going to trust Him to take good care of your other grandfather in his new world."

The story of the butterfly and the chrysalis is a simple one, and hearing it like Darren and his mother heard it in just the right circumstances gave them a tiny glimpse of eternity. It gives us a brief look at eternity, too.

I was acquainted with both grandfathers in this story. The grandpa, who had died, and I were teaching collegues at the same middle school. Like me, he experienced the loss of his first wife many years before. When my wife died, he offered to share his experience of recovery in a time of sorrow.

We had something else in common. His second wife was the librarian who worked with my second wife Norma Lee.

I don't know about you, but I want more than a glimpse of eternity. I want to see Eternity in all its glory with my loved ones and friends.

What is this eternity we have been talking about getting a tiny glimpse of? We can't tell anyone what eternity is like. We can't even prove there is an eternity to someone so that they will believe. We don't have to have an answer, but we can be an answer, just like Jesus! God doesn't just tell us the answers, He gave us Jesus to show us--Jesus is the answer. We can live our lives in such a way that God's love can be seen through us. When someone else can see God's love in us, we have opened the door to Eternity for them. Just think! We can be the instrument by which others will know how to live when they arrive there.

So, here we are, right back where we began. We came from love and we return to love. What a glorious thought to behold!

When we reach the stage of acceptnce in our recovery from the sorrow and grief of loss also comes hope. With hope also comes the promise of spending eternity with God. May we, like Darren, catch a glimpse of eternity.

Chapter Twenty
The Final Word

This has been the story of my life, or rather it is the account of how God's plan has unfolded in my life.

Links of Time has proven to my satisfaction that Jeremiah was indeed true when he said that God knew us before we were born; that He wanted nothing but the best for each one of us. His plan for us includes a desire for good with a hope for the future, a future of eternal life with Him.

Life is no bed of roses. No one is promised freedom from pain, sorrow, or suffering. How we deal with those times is up to the choices we make. My life has been no different than anyone else's. The death of two spouses, crippling polio, and chronic illnesses like diabetes and impending kidney failure are some of the most devastating events occurring in my life.

My ability to overcome the grief and adverse conditions, that have accompanied them, has helped me build a stronger faith in the knowledge that God does care and is always ready to help in time of need. This help most often has come through the lives of family members and close friends. There is no doubt in my mind, without them, my life would not have been the same.

God knew what his plan was for me. All I had to do was open the door. I am reminded of an artist's painting of Jesus standing outside the door waiting to be invited in. The scripture, John 3:19-21 says:

"Behold, I stand at the door and knock; if anyone hears my voice and opens the door, I will come in…"

One writer's creative observation says "The only key that unlocks the door is on the inside. The door cannot be opened from the outside." One of God's "angels", my neighbor Ray, was the key, opening the door a crack when he invited me to join the church choir of his church. From that beginning the door was soon opened wide. God used Ray to help carry out his plan for my life.

If it were possible to place all the tragic, disappointing episodes in my life on a scale with the beautiful memories of over 81 years--well, there would be no balance. My passion for music and teaching and my love for those who have been a source of recovery--especially family, friends, and two ladies named Norma, all far outweigh any of the down times in my life.

My greatest hope is that having been privileged to share my voice in singing, in teaching, and in my speaking from the pulpit, hopefully others have been able to grow stronger in their love of Christ, have found increased faith in the future, and eager to live in their hope of eternal life with the Father, just as I have.

Finally, let me quote those words that Norma Lee wrote to me on the night before our wedding. They are the closing lines of the poem quoted earlier.

*With **faith, hope** and **love**,*
all bound together.
Because of our feelings
and love for each other,
We'll go on ahead
with a full life together.

Yes, with Faith, Hope, and Love, all bound together, I can truly say that my life has been a life full of love beyond all measure. In spite of all the ups and downs of life I have experienced, it has been a wonderful adventure.

But now, I am looking forward to the greatest adventure of all. With a strong faith, and with hope in the future, I am looking forward to what happens when I come face to face with God. Someone once said, It's not hard to die when you know you have LIVED!

Jesus said it: *In my Father's house are many dwelling places. If it were not so, would I have told you that I go to prepare a place for you? I will come again and take you to myself so that where I am you may be also.*(Gospel of John 14:2-3, RSVB)

Afterwords

There's an oft-used saying that goes something like this: I am going to tell you what I am going to tell you. Then I am going to tell it to you. Finally, I am going to tell you what I told you.

In *Links of Time* I have tried to accomplish several things. What started out as an exploration of God's plan for my life, as recorded in the *Book of Jeremiah,* turned out to be a more complex set of ideas than one might imagine.

Though it might seem so to some, God's plan for each one of us is not to bring us adversity and pain and then expect us to seek relief through Jesus Christ's love. Instead, His plan is "for good, and not for evil, for a future and a hope." When a loss occurs in our lives, almost always something better is likely to come along to replace that loss. I have compared events in my life to links in a chain to explain how one was "attached" to the next. In the long run, the succeeding event most often helped me reach the stage of acceptance required for life to go on.

In retrospect, this pattern of events has been with me all my life. It was, however, that agonizing night of prayer which really started a whole new way of life for me--a life of singing, teaching, and speaking for God.

All of this, however, is prelude to something even more profound. After gathering all these ideas together, a deeper question arose in my mind. Why me? Why have I been so fortunate to have so many good things happen to me? Oh, yes, I have had a lot of pain and sorrow and loss in my life, some of which no one else can ever know. But such things have been far overshadowed by the beautiful people, events, and times in my life.

Willie Peterson expresses it best when he tells how the death of his wife was changing his life. From the Preface in my first book, *A Promise fulfilled*, comes the following story:

> A Denver Seminary professor, Willie Peterson, recently wrote an article [in 2000] on how the death of his wife was changing his life. He spoke about the loss of identity as a couple — "the two of us." He says he was forced to face the question of "who I am?" now that she was no longer there.
>
> He told of going from being a "self-assured proud male to the weeping bumbler" with a loss of self-confidence. He says how annoying it is to have his children trying to "supervise so many details of my life."
>
> The third thing he noted was the loss of "some measure of courage." Where he had always thought the two of them would face the challenges of the world together, now he realized that he was in a world of uncertainty alone.
>
> Finally, he recognized that this loss of identity, self-confidence, and courage were part of the grief process he was going through.
>
> Then he went on to say that he knew he was not alone or without support in this process. He wrote this: "God continues showing up in His people who have found creative and unbelievable patience to walk this path of grief with me. I don't expect the precious presence of the Lord to change as I move through my changes, losses, and fears."

The last paragraph containing Willie's quote has proved to be so true in my case. God has continued to find and send people into my life who have helped lift me out of the depression, sadness, and sorrow over time.

Still the question persists. Why me? Why does God care enough for me to make things turn out all right? One thought led to another. Suddenly, an even more meaningful way of stating the question is: No matter what you do in life, all that's important is What's in it for God?

Because he first loved me and because of his plan for my life, I am secure in the knowledge that he loves even me!

God's love for us is boundless. *We love because he first loved us.* (1John 4:19 NRSV)

.

Acknowledgements

My thanks to Larry Roberts for his faithfulness in weekly sharing time with me. His expert assistance in finalizing the *Links of Time* manuscript for publication and making the front cover graphics is also appreciated.

Thanks also to the staff and residents of the Leisure Care Retirement Community's Hawthorne Court facility for making it possible for me and all its residents to live life to the fullest possible.

Finally, thanks to members of my family, especially Teresa, who are always ready to answer my call whenever the need arises.

Without the loving care and concern
of these folks, and many others like them,
my life today would not be
what it has become.

For Further Reading

Aging With Dignity, *Five Wishes*. Copyright 2007. Aging With Dignity, PO Box 1661, Tallahassee, FL 32302.

Deits, Bob, *Life After Loss: A Personal Guide Dealing With Death, Divorce, Job Change,* and *Relocation*, Fisher Books, 1988, 1992

DelBene, Ron, *A Time To Mourn: Recovering From the Death Of a Loved One*. Copyright 1988 by Ron Del-Benem, Mary and Herb Montgomery

Guideposts, *Overcoming Grief – Stories of Enduring Faith*, Series *Comfort From Beyond*, Copyright 2004

Frankl, Victor E. *Man's Search For Meaning,* Washington Square Press, Copyright 1953.

Guideposts, *Until We Meet Again - Stories of Everlasting Love*, Series *Comfort From Beyond*, Copyright 2003

Kubler-Ross, Elisabeth, On Death and Dying. Copyright1969.

Kushner, Harold S., *When Bad Things Happen To Good People,* Copyright 1981 by Harold S. Kushner

Mayfield, James L., *Discovering Grace in Grief,* Upper Room Books, Copyright 1994.

Moore, James W., *When Grief Breaks Your Heart,,* Copyright 1995 By Abingdon Press

Peterson, Willie, *How the Death of My Wife is Changing My Life,* Focal Point Magazine, Vol. 20, Fall 2000, Denver Seminary (Used by permission of *Focal Point Magazine)*

Staudacher, Carol, *A Time To Grieve: Meditations For Healing After the Death of a Loved One*. Copyright 1994 by Carol Staudacher

Wilson, Janet, *Who Heals the Healer? Prominent Austin Pastor Comes to Terms with Wife's Death,* Austin

American Statesman, Copyright 2000.

Frankl, Victor E. *Man's Search For Meaning,* Washington Square Press, Copyright 1953.

OTHER BOOKS BY THE AUTHOR

Whitner, Richard G., *A Promise Fulfilled: How God Uses People,* Trafford Publishing, Copyright 2004 by Richard G. Whitner.

This book tells the story of how the writer over came adversity of several kinds, including the loss of two wives in death. With the help of many friends and loved ones, and the undergirding strength of his Christiian faith, a normal semblance of iufe was beginning to return. Writing this story was, in a large part, responsible for that to take place.

Richard G. Whitner, *From the Darkness Ibnto the Light. Moving from the Dariness Of Grief Into the Light of Hope, Trafford Publishing, copyright 2007 by Richrd G. Whitner*

Just when the writer was alsmot recovered from the grief experiences told in his first book, a terrible fall iresulted in a permanent life in a wheelchair. This book gives an account of how life was changed forever in an instant and how recovery of this, too, has come about.

Both books are available from Trafford Publishing, To order, toll-free 1-888-232-4444 (USA & Canada)
Phone 250 383 6864 and fax 812 355 4082

NOTES

Introduction & Back cover
Reprinted from *Winter Grace: Spirituality and Aging* by Kathleen Fischer. Copyright 1998 by Upper Room Books®. Used by permission from Upper Room Books®. To order, phone 1-800.972.0433 or www.upperroom.org/bookstore.

Chapter 1
From the Darkness Into the Light, pp. 8-9. By Richard G. Whitner. Copyright 2007 by Richard G. Whitner Used by permission. To order, phone 1-888-232-4444 9USA & Canada) email: info@trafford.com.

Kubler-Ross, Elisabeth, *On Death and Dying*. Copyright 1969. Macmillan, NY Used by permission

Chapter 14
Eeves, William O., Rev. *Arkansas United Method-ist,* United Methodist News Service, Copyright December 2004. Used by permission.

Chapter 17
Riesenweber, Patricia, *Wings For Eternity.* Used with permission of the author.

ABOUT THE AUTHOR

Richard George Whitner is a native of Yakima, WA, graduating from Yakima (Davis) Senior High School in 1947. He attended Yakima Valley Community College. During recovery from polio in 1952, he attended Yakima Business College. For fifteen years he worked as an office manager and accountant. During that time he worked with junior high age youth in his church. Because of this, a long-dormant desire to be a teacher was reawakened and he enrolled at Central Washington University in Ellensburg, WA in 1966, and graduated in the summer of 1969 with a B.A. Degree in Education. He began a teaching career lasting 23 years teaching U.S. history and English to seventh and eighth grade middle school students at Highlands Middle School, Kennewick, WA.

He is a United Methodist layperson and Certified Lay Speaker and served as a District and Conference Director of Lay Speaking Ministries for the Pacific Northwest Conference of the United Methodist Church. He has been a member of the West Highlands United Methodist Church congregation for almost 50 years, serving as its Lay Leader and Lay Member to Annual Conference for many of those years.

He enjoys writing as a hobby and was the editor of the church's *Newsletter* for over 30 years. *Links of Time* is his fourth book published by Trafford Publishing.

Richard now lives in a Leisure Care Retirement Community, Hawthorne Court's Assisted Living facility where he serves as the leader of the Resident Council.